D0732455

KHANIQAHI-NIMATULLAHI
(NIMATULLAHI SUFI ORDER)

306 West 11th Street
New York, New York 10014
Tele: 212-924-7739

4021 19th Avenue
San Francisco, California 94132
Tele: 415-586-1313

4931 MacArthur Blvd. NW
Washington, D.C. 20007
Tele: 202-338-4757

84 Pembroke Street
Boston, Massachusetts 02118
Tele: 617-536-0076

310 NE 57th Street
Seattle, Washington 98105
Tele: 206-527-5018

11019 Arleta Avenue
Mission Hills, Los Angeles, California 91345
Tele: 213-365-2226

4642 North Hermitage
Chicago, Illinois 60640
Tele: 312-561-1616

41 Chepstow Place
London W.2, England
Tele: 01-229-0769

IN THE
PARADISE
OF THE
SUFIS

IN THE PARADISE OF THE SUFIS

Dr. Javad Nurbakhsh

Translated from the Original Persian

KHANIQAHI-NIMATULLAHI PUBLICATIONS
NEW YORK

Also Available by Dr. Javad Nurbakhsh:

In the Tavern of Ruin: Seven Essays on Sufism
In the Paradise of the Sufis
What the Sufis Say
Masters of the Path
Divani Nurbakhsh: Sufi Poetry

Second Edition

Library of Congress Catalog Card Number: 79-83588

ISBN 0-933546-01-7

Cover Photograph: Tomb of Shah Ni'matullah Vali, Persian Sufi Saint (1330-1431), in Mahan, Iran.

PRINTED IN THE UNITED STATES OF AMERICA

CONTENTS

   I Tasavvuf: The Aim and Approach of Sufism
       (From a speech delivered at the American
       University of Beirut, 1967)   11

  II Zekr: The Heart of Sufi Practice   31

 III Fekr: The Sufi Way of Contemplation   53

 IV Moraqebeh: The Sufi Way of Meditation   71

  V Mohasebeh: The Sufi Way of Self-Examination 91

 VI Verd: The Sufi Way of Invocation   103

VII The Rules and Manners of Initiation into the
       Sufi Path   119

TASAVVUF

The Aim
and Approach of Sufism

THE CRAZY INTELLECT

Through Love, I have reached a place
where no trace of Love remains,
Where 'I' and 'we' and the painting of existence
have all been forgotten and left behind.

Now who can know where I am,
here where no knowledge, no opinion can be found.
Here even Love is bewildered
and the intellect is crazy, talking nonsense.

Totally impoverished, I have no wealth,
no identity, no self—
Free from faithfulness and faithlessness,
a stranger to myself and all acquaintances.

Yet only for this can I still be blamed—
that a cry comes from me,
Out of grief for Nurbakhsh I say,
"You have gone. How is it I know not where?"

IN THE NAME OF THE MOST EXALTED AND SACRED

THE DEFINITION OF SUFISM

Sufism is a school of spiritual states, not discourse; and a sufi is something to become, not something to merely read about.

Since spiritual states cannot be expressed in words, sufi shaikhs have declared, "Whatever can be expressed in words is not sufism." As Rumi has put it:

> *When I come to Love, I am ashamed of all*
> *That I have ever said about Love.*

Whatever great sufis have said in explanation of *tasavvuf* (sufism) was the result of and appropriate to their particular situations and states. Such explanations, therefore, do not constitute general definitions of sufism. Rather, they refer to some of the characteristics of sufism.

What can be considered, to some extent, a general definition of *tasavvuf* is this:

> *Sufism is a path towards the Truth where the provisions are Love. Its method is to look solely in one direction, and its objective is God.*

At the end of the sufi path, nothing remains but God.

The aim of sufism is the realization of the Truth. Although philosophers consider that such an aim is achieved using reason and a process of logic or argument, the realization of the Truth is truly possible only with the eye of the heart and the conscience, through a process of unveiling and illumination. Thus, sufism means going and seeing, not sitting and talking.

WHO IS THE SUFI?

The sufi is one who moves towards the Truth by means of Love and devotion. He or she knows that the realization of the Truth is only possible for the Perfected One, for in a state of imperfection human beings are unable to recognize the Truth. Imperfection can be seen as an abnormal condition in which one's ability to see things as they really are is deficient. An imperfect being, by virtue of his imperfection, misperceives the Truth without being aware of it, and therefore his understanding of the Truth is unconsciously mistaken.

In the view of the sufi, what is known as the 'commanding self' (*nafs-e ammareh*), which resides in the unconscious, closely monitors and dominates the thoughts and behavior of each individual. Consequently, one's ability to discriminate is clouded by the desires and attachments of the 'commanding self', and discrimination is necessarily faulty.

SUFIOLOGISTS

Those who study sufism and derive their own interpretations are called *motasavvefeh,* or 'sufiologists'. Although such people may possess a great deal of information about sufi characteristics, they do not really know the sufis. They do not have sufi characteristics themselves, nor can they know what the sufi *sees* with the eye of the heart. Therefore, their statements about sufism will probably not be authoritative for sufis, although they might be very interesting from the point of view of defining sufism.

Since only one who is perfect is capable of realizing the Truth, the sufi strives his utmost for Perfection. For sufis, the model and manifestation of the Perfected One in the external world is 'Ali ibn Abi Taleb, the cousin of the Prophet of Islam. Also, all the sufi masters and shaikhs were beings who realized varying degrees of Perfection.

The question arises why 'Ali as a disciple of the Prophet should be considered the model of the Perfected One, rather than the Prophet himself. Sufis do, indeed, believe that the Prophet is the supreme manifestation of Perfection. But the Prophet's Perfection was a gift of God, whereas 'Ali achieved Perfection and mastership through being a disciple of the Prophet. It is from the perspective of his discipleship that he provides the model for sufis.

Conceptually, the Perfected One is an individual who has become freed from the dictates of the 'commanding self' (*nafs-e ammareh*). Both inwardly and outwardly, such a being is the manifestation of the Divine Attributes. Having become one with the Absolute, he is freed from the relativity of 'I' and 'we'. He is a mirror which perfectly reflects God. When one looks upon him, one sees nothing but the Truth.

Is it possible to become a Perfected One? The answer is "Yes".

Sufis believe that the only way to become perfect is to purify oneself under the training of a perfect master. This course of training is called the *tariqat* (Spiritual Path). In order to undertake such training, however, one must first follow the *shari'at* (the religious precepts constituting Islamic Law). At the end of the *tariqat,* one arrives at the threshold of the *haqiqat* (the Truth). As the Prophet has said, "The *shari'at* is my words, the *tariqat* my actions, and the *haqiqat* my states."

One who enters the *tariqat* is called a *morid,* while the master of the *tariqat* is known as the *morad.*

SEEKING (TALAB)

The attraction towards God, indeed, all movement forward on the Path, is due to the Will of God alone, as expressed in the *Qur'an*

(2:272) where God tells the Prophet, "It is not you who are responsible for guiding them, for God guides whom He wills." This attraction towards God is called *talab,* which means both 'calling' from God's direction and 'seeking' from man's. *Talab* is the force which aids and encourages the disciple during his movement towards Perfection. It generates in him a feeling of dissatisfaction with his present condition, compelling him to seek a state of peace.

Although this compulsion is God at work within the seeker, it is equally vital to have a master as the outward manifestation of God's Will. This is based upon the *Qur'anic* passage in which God tells the Prophet, "You are the guide on the straight path." (42:52)

Eventually, *talab* leads the disciple to experience peace of mind and a growing sense of security and tranquility. In the higher stages, *talab* becomes the seeking for eternal Beauty, Goodness, and Perfection which it wants to possess forever.

SPIRITUAL POVERTY (FAQR)

The feeling of seeking (*talab*) is a manifestation of what is known as Spiritual Poverty (*faqr*). One who possesses such Spiritual Poverty is referred to as 'an impoverished one' (*faqir*). Spiritual Poverty is a state born of a sense of need, giving rise to the search for a remedy. The *faqir* feels 'empty-handed', that he lacks the higher attributes which are man's potential. Thus, he is moved to set about finding a way to amend this feeling or 'neediness'.

THE DISCIPLE (MORID)

The relationship between the master and disciple pertains to the intermediate phase of the Spiritual Path. The goal of the Spiritual Path is for the self of the traveler to become transformed from the 'commanding self' (*nafs-e ammareh*), to the 'blaming or reproving self' (*nafs-e lavvameh*), and finally to the 'self-at-rest' (*nafs-e motma'eneh*).The motivation of the 'commanding self' is to satisfy its animal instincts and desires. The 'reproving self' blames the 'commanding self' for this and seeks Perfection. The 'self-at-rest' has found peace and come to Perfection. At this point, the disciple is

worthy of attending the banquet of Unity and being in the Divine
Presence, as referred to in the *Qur'anic* verse, "O Self-at-Rest, return
to your Lord, well-pleased (with Him), (and) He well-pleased with
thee." (89:28)

While traveling the Path and observing its 'rules and manners'
(*adab*[1]), the disciple is freed from the pressure of psychological
conflicts. He is cleansed of egotistical qualities, and the energy that
was previously taken up in worldly distractions is now used to polish
the heart and mind. At the end of the Path, the disciple is emptied of
the attributes of the self and adorned by the Divine Attributes. Such a
being has truly put into practice the saying of the Prophet, "Make
yourself in harmony with the Divine Nature."

As Hafez has expressed it:

Purify thyself, and then proceed
to the 'Tavern of Ruin'.

The purification referred to here is the purifying of the heart which
takes place during the course of the *tariqat* (Spiritual Path), while the
'Tavern of Ruin' represents the 'passing away of the self in God' (*fana*),
which is considered part of the final stage of *tasavvuf,* or the Truth
(*haqiqat*).

In the initial phase of the Path, the disciple undergoes a process
of confirming his faith in the master and gaining assurance that the
master can take him to the final aim of human Perfection. The master
during this phase determines that the seeker has proceeded with
sincerity and devotion and is deserving of his guidance.

Once the master and disciple have accepted one another, the
master assures the disciple that all of his previous misbehavior will be
forgiven provided that from then on he does not engage in what has
been prohibited. From the sufi point of view, the initiation into the
tariqat is a second birth for the disciple. As Jesus has said, "He who
enters not into the angelic kingdom of the heavens and earth is one who
has not been born again." Sufis believe that an initiated person is born

---

1. *adab:* a term that has various meanings depending upon the context in which it is used.
Accordingly, it may be translated as 'rules of behavior', 'how to be (or behave)', 'etiquette',
'politeness', 'culture', 'civilization', 'decorum', 'good manners'. For the sake of brevity, *adab* has
been translated as 'rules and manners' throughout this book (ed.).

twice: once from his mother and once again into the world of Love, Loving-kindness, Devotion, and Unity.

The initial phase of the Path generally takes from seven to twelve years. In the words of Hafez:

> *The aim of shepherd Moses*
> *of the Promised Land*
> *Was reached with years of service*
> *at master Sho'eib's hand.*

THE MASTER (MORAD)

The master is a Perfected One who has at the very least completed all phases of the Path. Being a master is not something to be merely claimed; it must be attained through training under a perfect master. The true master is linked to the spiritual chain of masters which extends back to the Prophet.

Traveling the Path can be done in two ways:

1. By means of Divine Grace—wherein God seizes one of his devotees and takes him away from himself, granting him His Presence. A person carried away in this manner is called *majzub,* or 'an enraptured one'. But this is a rare occurrence.

2. By means of discipleship—being a traveler (*salek*) on the Path. This is the way of striving, as expressed in the *Qur'anic* passage, "Those who strive towards Us, certainly shall We guide them in Our ways." (29:69)

One who has achieved the end in only one of these ways, as either *majzub* or *salek,* cannot be a master. A master must have gone from the state of 'enrapturement' (*jazbeh*) to that of 'traveling' (*soluk*), or the reverse. Neither state alone is Perfection, and the master must be Perfect.

In short, the master must have traveled the Path and come to know the Path before he can lead others on the way.

The true disciple is one who witnesses in his heart the spiritual beauty of the master and immediately falls in love with this beauty. Being such a lover is the source of all blessings. Until the disciple has fallen in love with the Divine Beauty of the master, he cannot become surrendered to the master's will. In truth, the disciple is one who surrenders to the master's will, not one who remains the disciple of his own will.

> *O heart, if you want the Beloved to be content,*
> *do and say whatever He desires.*
> *If He says cry tears of blood, don't ask why,*
> *and if He says give up your soul, don't ask the*
> *reason.*

The first step then, after choosing a master and becoming inspired with faith in him, is to obey his instructions without questioning "how" or "why".

> *On the way to the Beloved Layla's abode,*
> *there are many dangers and risks.*
> *Unless you are an insane lover like Majnun,*
> *you won't take even a single step.*

Whatever the master orders, even if it is not immediately clear to the disciple, should be carried out. As Hafez has said:

> *Stain your prayer rug with wine*
> *If the Master of the Holy Fire so commands.*

The same point is illustrated in the *Qur'anic* story of Moses and Khezr in which Moses asks Khezr (the master of the Path) for

18 permission to become his disciple and is told, "If thou followest me, ask me about nothing until I myself mention it to you." (18:70)

Besides unquestioningly following the master's instructions, the disciple should do nothing of importance without the permission of the master. He should reveal to no one the secrets that exist between himself and the master. Moreover, whatever the disciple witnesses in his dream or waking states should be confided only to the master.

The disciple should never try to challenge the master in any pursuit. As the *Qur'an* (49:1) says, "O you who believe, be not forward in the presence of God and His Prophet." That is, the disciple should always try to be humble before the master and not manifest his 'self'. He should not venture an opinion unless he is invited to do so, nor should he perform any action unless he is so directed. It is in reference to this that it has been said, "Love is but an Ethic," to which may be added, ". . .and the Path is merely the observance of that Ethic."

In accordance with the *Qur'anic* passage (49:2), "O you who believe, do not raise your voices above the voice of the Prophet," the disciple should never speak loudly in the presence of the master, for "the master amongst his followers is like the Prophet in his community."

THE COURSE OF THE PATH

The disciple's development falls into two stages. In the first, he undergoes a process of resolving psychological conflicts and lessening the control of the self until he reaches a state of psychological harmony, equilibrium, and peace of mind. In the second, the disciple undergoes a process of becoming illuminated by the Divine Attributes and Divine Nature.

From the viewpoint of modern psychotherapy, during the initial stage of the Path the master observes and studies the behavior of the disciple. In this process, as in psychotherapy, the interpretation of dreams and visions plays an important role. The disciple relates his dreams and visions to the master, who, understanding their meaning and significance, sees the disciple's inner conflicts and compulsions

and undertakes to cure him of them. It is important here that the
disciple refrain from speaking about his dreams and visions to anyone
other than the master.

In this way, the first stage of the Path is properly psycho-
theraputic, varying in length according to the individual's own
particular psychological condition. Modern psychotherapy is, in fact,
an imperfect imitation of the sufi approach since it lacks spiritual
content. The curative process of sufism results in the purification not
only of the mind, but of the heart. With the elixir of Love, the master
liberates the disciple from self-centered qualities and opens him to the
manifestations of the Divine Attributes.

In the beginning of the Path, the disciple should adhere to the
following instructions:

1. Observance of Islam;

2. Cultivation of kindness towards God's creatures;

3. Maintenance of discretion concerning the secrets of the Path,
both with respect to fellow darvishes and to outsiders;

4. Obedience to the rules of the Path.

Once the master sees that the disciple is ready to undertake the
procedure of the *tariqat*, he inculcates the *zekr* in him.

ZEKR (REMEMBRANCE OF THE DIVINE NAMES)

The *zekr* of the sufis is a Name of God transmitted to the disciple
in a special manner by the master of the Path. Through the inculcation
of *zekr*, the master instructs the disciple how to be in continuous
remembrance of the Divine.

So much He sat facing my open heart,
My heart was imbued with His nature and ways.

When the disciple is continually involved in the remembrance of God,
his being gradually becomes liberated from egotistical and selfish
qualities and illuminated by the Divine Attributes and Divine Nature.

In the beginning, the purpose of remembering God is to create a 'unity of attention'. Until this is attained, the disciple will be attentive to the various attachments of the self. Therefore, he should try to incline his scattered attention to the all-encompassing point of Unity.

The remembrance of God effaces the memory of all other things, and the energy that was previously dispersed in worthless and short-term concerns now finds its proper focus in the remembrance of God. At the same time, psychological conflicts are reduced, leading to peace of mind in the disciple.

In the course of remembrance, the sufi is attentive to the Name itself, as well as to its meaning or significance. This is necessary since human beings have the habit of being attentive to a concept by means of words. Thus, when a word is remembered, the corresponding concept tends to arise in one's awareness. Attention to the Name alone, however, is a kind of idol-worship, for the word itself has no special properties. Of course, in the beginning, the disciple has no alternative but to focus on the words of the remembrance, coming gradually to the association of form and meaning until he is able to dispense with the form of the words altogether.

I will pass away from word, utterance and act,
so without these three, I can be with You.

Rumi

Sufis believe that the disciple in remembrance should forget not only this world and the one after, but himself as well. As long as the disciple is conscious of himself in the course of remembrance, he is regarded as being in a state of infidelity.

The *zekr* of the sufis, then, is like a flood which gradually eliminates the self-centered qualities and illuminates the Divine Attributes in the disciple's heart. Ultimately, the very illusion of 'self' also becomes swept away and taken by the flood. This marks the end of the Path and the beginning of the ocean of selflessness.

Yet the remembrance by itself is not sufficient to achieve this end. Devotion to the master is what really brings about the aim. Until the sense of devotion has overwhelmed the disciple, the tree of *zekr* cannot bring forth the fruit of *fana* ('passing away of the self in God').

Sufis believe that the Names of God have no limit—each Name representing an Attribute, each Attribute evoking an understanding, and each understanding effecting a realization of the Divine Omnipresence. The transcendent quality of each Attribute shines before the eyes of one who is devoted to God and brings peace upon him according to his individual capacity. Each time an Attribute is revealed to him through a flash of light from the window of a Divine Name, his ardor and longing increase. [2]

MIRACLES AND POWERS

The true sufi is not concerned with miracles and spiritual powers. He makes no claim of being the source of miracles or of possessing powers beyond those which human beings normally possess. Since the sufi negates everything but God, he considers such claims to be manifestations of *being,* or affirmations of a separate existence apart from God. That is, the sufi regards the self as relative in relation to the absoluteness of God, and considers all acts and intuitions issuing from the self as obstacles to receiving the grace of God.

Some people mistakenly imagine that sufi masters claim to possess spiritual powers or to perform miracles. However, sufi masters themselves make no such claims. Rather, it is the disciple who, by virtue of his devotion, may see miraculous or spiritual powers in the master or shaikh. At certain stages, therefore, it may be necessary for the master to liberate the disciple from this idol-worshipping frame of mind and lead him back to the cognizance of God.

FREE WILL AND DETERMINATION

At the beginning of the Path, according to sufis, free will (*tafviz*) is the predominating factor since the disciple is still entangled in the conflicts of the self. At this point, the disciple is largely influenced by the dictates of the self's desires which overwhelm the individual will. In

2. This process is described most fully in Kashani's *Mesbahol-Hedayeh.*

accordance with the *Qur'anic* verse (53:39), "Man has nought but what he strives for," the disciple should apply his own will here in order to become emptied of his self's compulsions and to prepare himself to fully manifest the Divine Attributes. This process can take place only through individual striving combined with Divine Attraction. According to Hafez:

> *Although Union with the Beloved*
> *Is never given as a reward for one's efforts,*
> *Strive, O heart, as much as you are able.*

At the end of the disciple's traveling, with the 'passing away of individual action' (*fana-ye af'al*) and the illumination of the Divine Attributes in his inner being, the disciple sees that everything is determined (*jabr*). Here, there is no more interposition of 'I' or 'we'; all that the sufi does or wills is that which God does or wills.

SOLITUDE WHILE IN SOCIETY

Sufis consider idleness and laziness a disgrace, and concern themselves as much as possible with service to the society in which they live. In this way, they serve God's creation externally while within they are preoccupied with God alone. As Sa'di has expressed it:

> *Have you ever heard of one*
> *who is absent and present at the same time?*
> *'Tis I, who am in the crowd*
> *while my heart has gone beyond.*

The greatest discipline for the sufi is to live harmoniously among people. This is considered to be a sign of human Perfection. In contrast, one who is unable to have such harmony is considered to be imperfect. In the view of the sufi, Perfection can be attained only in society. It is in this regard that the expression 'inner journey and outward manner' has been used, indicating that the inner spiritual journey is not enough to take one to Perfection. Perfection can be

realized only when one's actions are in harmony with God's creation
and one's inner being is focused solely upon God.

The sufi is not only kind and of service to others, but he is also not offended by their ego-oriented behavior. Society is the touchstone of Perfection for the sufi—whenever he become offended and acts reproachfully towards behavior directed against him, he has fallen into infidelity. As Hafez has said:

> *We bear reproach with joy, remaining faithful,*
> *For taking offense at another's acts*
> *Is infidelity on the Beloved's way.*

One who is unfaithful in this manner is caught up in duality, for he perceives God and himself as separate entities.

In other words, sufis do not retreat from society and practice solitude. When people say that sufis cultivate asceticism and reject society, it should be understood that it is only when the master diagnoses a condition of psychological imbalance in a disciple that he may prescribe solitude and, in addition, a vegetarian diet. Moreover, such a regimen is maintained only until the disciple recovers his balance.

Abstinence and solitude then are not principles of sufism. That is to say, they are not disciplines leading to spiritual Perfection. Rather, they are instructions to cure a temporary condition of imbalance. In fact, since service to others and attention to God consume energy, the sufi knows that a proper diet is required. The intake of food, however, is not in itself of value. It is only the use of the energy provided that has importance. In the words of Rumi:

> *One eats and turns his nurture into Godly light.*
> *Another eats and nurtures avarice and spite.*

FANA AND BAQA

The end of the Spiritual Path (*tariqat*), of traveling towards God, is the spiritual station (*maqham*) of *fana* ('passing away of the self in God').[3] There are two kinds of fana : outer and inner.

---

3. For the difference between 'station' (*maqham*) and 'state' (*hal*), see "Sayings of the Great Sufis" in the chapter *Mohasebeh* (ed.).

The outer fana is the 'passing away of individual action' (*fana-ye af'al*), with the resulting manifestation of Divine Action. The one who reaches this station becomes drowned in the Ocean of Divine Action, so that he perceives in all events the Action and Will of God, seeing neither himself nor any other individual as one who does or wills any event. He becomes so completely without will that no trace of willing any individual action remains in him.

The inner fana involves the 'passing away of the attributes of the self' (*fana-ye sefat*) and the 'passing away of the essence of the self' (*fana-ye zat*). Sometimes, in discovery of the Divine Attributes, the possessor of this state (*hal*) becomes drowned in the passing away of his own attributes. At other times, in witnessing the exalted effects of the Divine Essence, he becomes drowned in the passing away of his essence.

In the beginning of this inner fana, the sufi loses his senses. Gradually, according to his capacity, the condition of being both absent and present at the same time descends upon him. Inwardly he is drowned in the ocean of fana, while outwardly he participates in the events around him.

There are many examples of sufis experiencing this condition. It is reported that 'Ali was once struck in the leg by an arrow in the course of battle. His companions tried to remove it but failed because the arrow had penetrated so deeply. Asking the Prophet's advice, they were told to take out the arrow while 'Ali was in prayer, which they then did easily. In another account, the sufi Moslem ibn Yasar was praying in the congregational mosque of Basra when a supporting column collapsed. The sound it made was so loud that everyone in the bazaar outside heard it. Yet ibn Yasar, in the mosque itself, was unaware of what had transpired.

Baqa is the beginning of the 'journey in God'. Having caused the passing away of the disciple's will, God endows such a slave with His Will, so that whatever the slave wills is now the Will of the Divine. This baqa corresponds to the outer fana.

The baqa corresponding to the inner fana, however, is one in which the very veils that are the temporary essence and attributes of the disciple's self are removed. Here, God neither veils the creation, nor does the creation veil God. The veil has been totally removed, and duality transformed into Unity.

O darvish, human beings of every nation and religion all exist by the honorable cloak of existence; all are human beings like you. If you are truly a lover of Absolute Being, love all beings and be kind to them. By doing so, you prove that you deserve the privilege of belonging to the human family.

O darvish, disrespect for what others hold sacred only indicates your own imperfection. In this regard, try to make yourself perfect in the eyes of those who truly see.

O darvish, you have entered your name in the book of outstanding human beings. If you are not capable of becoming one of these people, try not to disgrace those few who truly hold the good name of 'sufi'.

O darvish, if anyone behaves badly towards you, do not consider him a bad person. Look upon him as one who has a sickness and be kind to him. If you conduct yourself in this way, you truly possess health of the spirit.

There are five principles that darvishes of the Nimatullahi Order should put into practice:

Zekr   (Remembrance)

Fekr   (Contemplation)

Moraqebeh   (Meditation)

Mohasebeh   (Self-Examination)

Verd   (Invocation)

ZEKR

The Heart
of Sufi Practice

THE NAME OF THE FRIEND

Say always the name of the Friend, slowly, slowly;
with this alchemy change the copper of the heart into gold
slowly, slowly

Drink from the wine of union in the tavern of Unity
so that 'I' and 'you' will be taken from your mind
slowly, slowly

Stamp your foot on the head of existence, empty your hands
of both worlds,
and you'll become a confidant of God's secret
slowly, slowly.

Seek a road from that king who has the "wealth of Allah",*
and sooner or later he will separate you from yourself
slowly, slowly.

In Love's district impatience brings loss, since difficulties
will be made easy by surrender and contentment
slowly, slowly.

There are thousands of tests in store for a sincere lover,
all so that he will come to know Love's secret
slowly, slowly.

The knower of God who strives truly will travel the stations
of the way;
he'll travel the road of baqa *after the road of* fana
slowly, slowly.

In the school of lovers, silence is better than speech.
O Nurbakhsh, this statement was made clear
slowly, slowly.

*Ni'matullah

HE IS THE REMEMBERER AND THE REMEMBERED

Happiest were the times spent with the Beloved;
The rest were vain and fruitless.

Hafez

THE DEFINITION OF ZEKR

Zekr is defined in the dictionary as 'remembrance'. However, the word *zekr* has also been used to mean:

1. The contrary of forgetfulness.

2. Utterances and remembrance with the tongue.

3. An imprinting on the mind in a way that is permanent and unforgettable.

4. A particular expression that has descended from the Divine into the heart, such as is found in the prayers (*namaz*) and invocation (*verd*) of spiritual practice.

5. Awareness of one's actions.

6. Remembrance of the heart.

7. Preservation.

8. Obedience and rewards.

9. Daily prayer.

32 10. Expression.

11. Traditions (*Ahadith*).

12. *Qur'an.*

13. Knowledge.

14. Nobility.

15. Thankfulness.

16. Friday prayers.

17. Evening prayers.

THE MEANING OF ZEKR

According to sufis, zekr is the total and uncompromised attention to God, ignoring all that is not God.

You remember Us truly in your heart and soul,
Only when you have forgotten both the worlds.

Shah Ni'matullah Vali

Confirming this view is the *Qur'anic* passage (18:24), "Remember your Lord when you are forgetful. . . ." Although this passage has been interpreted to mean, "Remember your Lord when you are forgetful. . .of Him," some masters have said that its true interpretation is, "You remember your Lord only when you have forgotten everything else."

According to Imam Ja'far Sadeq:

Remembering repentance at the time of remembering God is forgetting the remembrance of God. To truly remember God is to forget all that is other than God, for God has priority over the sum of all things.

(cited by Attar, *Tales of the Saints*)

The sufi text *Shar-e Ta'rof* states, "The true meaning of zekr is to forget everything other than the Remembered." And Khwajeh 'Abdollah Ansari has written, "Zekr is freeing oneself from negligence and forgetfulness."

It has been said that zekr is sitting and waiting for acceptance by the Divine after detachment from man. To put it in another way, the sign of a lover is the constant remembrance of the Beloved.

Ahmad Khazruyeh was asked, "What is the sign of being a lover?" He replied, "There should be nothing of the two worlds which is greater in one's heart than the remembrance of the Beloved."

ZEKR IN THE QUR'AN

Many verses occur in the *Qur'an* about zekr, such as:

Turn away from the one who turns his back on
remembrance of Us, who seeks only the life of this world.
(53:29)

When you are not in prayer, remember God standing and
sitting and lying down. (4:103)

Remember your Lord's Name and devote yourself to Him
whole-heartedly. (73:8)

Remember your Lord over and over; exalt Him at daybreak
and in the dark of the night. (3:40)

Remember the Name of your Lord in the morning and in
the evening. (76:25)

O you who believe, remember God again and again. (33:41)

Remember God over and over; thus you may be successful.
(62:10)

Verily, prayer restrains one from evil, and certainly the
remembrance of God is greatest. (29:45)

One can recite the words of zekr heard from anyone, but zekr itself can be bestowed only by a perfect master. To receive zekr in the first manner is like catching a seed scattered by the wind. As Rumi has expressed it:

> *All know this existence is a trap,*
> *Yet zekr born of the will*
> *Only paves the road to hell.*

To receive zekr in the second manner, from a perfect master, is like having the seed planted in fertile soil. Under the care and nurturing of a perfect master, the seed of zekr planted in the heart will take root, grow, and bear fruit.

Zekr handed down by a perfect master can be divided into two types: 'vocal zekr' (*zekr-e jali*) and 'zekr of the heart' (*zekr-e khafi*). *Zekr-e jali* refers to zekr that is said vocally, and generally in a loud voice. This zekr takes place in sufi gatherings or in the sufi khaniqah. In this instance, the sufis gather together in a circle and chant the 'vocal zekr' harmoniously under the direction of the master of the *tariqat*. *Zekr-e jali* is regularly practiced by such orders as the Qaderi. Other sufi orders, however, prefer 'zekr of the heart'.

In the beginning, it is recommended that disciples pay attention to the utterance of the Name, while at the same time attempting to attend to the significance of the Name. The utterance of the Name is necessary for awakening the heart since the heart of the beginner is more easily awakened by the utterance than by the meaning. Thus, in the early stages of the Path, the master encourages 'vocal zekr'. However, as the heart gradually becomes familiar with that which is being remembered, it ceases to need 'vocal zekr'. Although *zekr-e jali* is sometimes practiced in the presence of the shaikh during gatherings of the Nimatullahi Order, it is *zekr-e khafi* that is stressed.

Zekr-e khafi or *qalbi* (also 'of the heart') is zekr integrated with the rhythm of breathing such that not a single breath passes without zekr. With *zekr-e khafi,* there is no need for a special gathering; moreover, no utterance is necessary.

Some masters have described zekr as spiritual wine, saying that

zekr-e jali is like spilling the wine down your shirt-front, while *zekr-e*
khafi is like drinking the wine and getting drunk.

> *There is no grace for the heart and soul*
> *in the zekr of the tongue.*
> *Spiritual wine will not rob your reason*
> *if you pour it down your shirt.*

Many verses of the *Qur'an* and Traditions of the Prophet speak
of *zekr-e khafi:*

Remember your Lord in your heart, humbly and with awe
and without utterance, at dawn and at dark, and be not
amongst the neglectful. (7:205)

The hearts of those who believe are set at rest by God's
remembrance; indeed, by God's remembrance (only) are
hearts set at rest. (13:28)

Be patient with those who call unto their Lord, morning and
evening, seeking His pleasure. Indeed, do not turn your eyes
from them, as if you were attracted merely to the veneer of
the life of the world. Do not follow the one whose heart We
have turned from Our remembrance and who follows his
own desires and wanders from his purpose. (18:28)

The highest remembrance is *zekr-e khafi.* (Saying of the
Prophet, cited by Ruzbehan in the *Mashrabol-arvah*)

Said God, the most Mighty and Precious, 'For one who
remembers Me inwardly, I remember him outwardly.'
(Imam Hosein, cited by Koleini in *Osul-e Kafi*)

Said God, the most Mighty and Precious, 'I take form in
the thought of My worshipper, and I am with him when he
remembers Me. If he remembers Me inwardly, I will
remember him inwardly, and if he remembers Me
outwardly, I will remember him outwardly, for My
remembrance is the greater. . .' (a tradition cited by Shah
Ni'matullah Vali, first book of the *Complete Works*)

He who remembers God, the most Mighty and Precious, inwardly, truly remembers Him over and over. Verily, they were hypocrites who remembered God outwardly, but not inwardly. The *Qur'an* says, '. . .They deceived the people and remembered God but little.' (Sayings of 'Ali)

When God says, 'Remember your Lord in your heart, humbly and with awe,' even the angel who records it knows not the merit of that remembrance in a person's heart, for it is so great that only God can know it. (*Osul-e Kafi*)

O Lord, busy our hearts with remembrance of You above all other remembrances and occupy our tongues with thanks to You above all other thankfulness. O Lord, open my heart to Your Loving-kindness, and fill me with Your Remembrance. (Imam Zeinol-'abedin, *Sahifeh-ye sajjadieh*)

THE RULES AND MANNERS (ADAB) OF ZEKR

1. The disciple should at all times be purified by ablution (*wozu*[1]).

2. He (or she) should wear clean clothes.

3. He should have a good aroma.

4. He should sit facing the *Qiblah* (the direction of Islamic prayer toward Mecca).

5. It is recommended that he sit with the eyes closed.

6. In the course of zekr, he should appeal internally for the master's help.

7. The disciple should sit on the knees with the legs folded under, placing the palm of the right hand on the left thigh and grasping the right wrist with the left hand. In this manner, the legs and arms both

---

1. *wozu:* the ritual washing performed before saying daily prayers (*namaz*) in Islam (ed.).

form the word 'la', which in Arabic means 'no' or 'not'. This
position stresses the sufi's nothingness and the negation of his sense
of 'I-ness'. Thus, his body is in harmony with his inner state which is
the negation of the 'self'.

8. The sufi should empty his heart of everything but God,
forgetting even his very self and focusing his attention completely on
God. For example, he omits the vocative particle 'Ya' ('O' in English)
in invoking God's Name. Thus, instead of saying "Ya Haqq" ("O
God"), he says just, "Haqq". The sufi in the state of zekr is not
aware of himself as a separate entity which could call upon another.
One who is aware of self in the state of zekr is no better than a liar.

9. The disciple should try to remain silent, speaking no more than is
necessary.

10. The sufi in zekr should not object to whatever condition descends
upon him, whether spiritual contraction or expansion, sickness or
health, pleasure or pain. He accepts all conditions equally and is
content, never turning away from God.

TRADITIONS OF THE IMAMS CONCERNING THE INCULCATION OF ZEKR

It is related that the Prophet of Islam once gathered a group of
the elect Companions privately into a house. He then spoke about the
basic zekr of Islam, *La ilaha illa'llah* (There is no god but God),
asking them to repeat it aloud with him. When this was done three
times, he raised his hands, crying, "O God, did this pass your
approval?" After a moment's pause, he told the Companions, "Good
tidings to you that God blesses you." (*Mersadol-ebad*)
From that time, sufi masters have followed the Prophet's
example of inculcating zekr in their disciples.
'Ali once asked the Prophet to show him the shortest and easiest
path to God. The Prophet told him to recite the zekr of God in solitude.
'Ali asked, "How should I practice zekr?" The Prophet said, "Close
your eyes and listen to me saying *La ilaha illa'llah.*" 'Ali listened to
the Prophet repeat the zekr three times; then the Prophet listened to 'Ali
say it three times in turn. (*Javaher-e Khamseh*)

38   Masters maintain that each zekr handed down to their disciples
comes through a chain of initiation originating with the Prophet and
'Ali.

HOW ZEKR TAKES EFFECT

> *Remembrance of the Divine is not the job*
> *of a useless idler,*
> *And return to God is not the way*
> *of any worthless wanderer.*
>
> *Rumi*

Three conditions are necessary for zekr to have its effect:

1.   The seed of zekr should be nourished by the Loving-kindness
(*mohabbat*) which issues through the master.

2.   The terrain of the sufi's heart should be furrowed by the plow of
devotion.

3.   The plant which grows from the seed must be tended by the
master until it bears the fruit of Loving-kindness in the disciple.

The zekr which has been inculcated by a master who is in the true
'chain of succession of masters' is the fruit of the tree of Loving-
kindness. Such a zekr is like a fertile seed ready to be sown. If the zekr
comes from a master not in this succession, however, it is like a
defective seed which, though planted in the disciple's heart, has little
chance of growing. Moreover, even if it should grow, it would be
vulnerable to pestilence and disease.
     The seed of Loving-kindness which is planted in the sufi's heart is
nurtured and protected from pestilence through the attention of the
master, for the true master has traveled the Path and seen the dangers
that threaten the traveler. He knows how to deal with each situation in

which the seed of Loving-kindness and Devotion is endangered, and is able to foster it so that it may grow safely to maturity and bear fruit. Zekr is the spiritual connection between master and disciple. By means of his connection to the master, the disciple from the earliest stages becomes linked to God. Thus, the disciple who lacks devotion to his master cannot benefit from the zekr which the master has given him.

On the other hand, a master who lacks a link with the Divine and is not the manifestation of God's Perfection will merely lead his disciples into egotism and self-worship rather than devotion to God.

THE RESULTS AND FRUIT OF ZEKR

While the distractions of the senses can be overcome through observance of the *shari'at,* the distractions of the self (*nafs*) which darken and agitate the heart can be averted only by the devoted practice of zekr—a practice based upon the negation of the thought of everything but God. When the light of zekr clears the heart of the darkness of agitation, the heart becomes aroused and gradually steals the zekr from the tongue, making it its preoccupation.

Zekr rends all the veils that are woven by the self's desires and attachments. As the darkness of the heart is lessened, these veils are removed and the light of zekr shines fully upon the heart. At the same time, however, anxiety is also created in the heart. This anxiety is not fear; it is the dread of losing this new-found state and returning to the previous one. It is an anxiety mixed with eagerness, enthusiasm, and hope. In reference to this, the *Qur'an* states, "Verily, the believers are those upon whose hearts fear descends when God's Name is remembered." (8:2)

By the water of zekr, the harshness and aggressiveness in the heart become washed away and are replaced with smoothness and softness. By the light of zekr, the darkness which frightens and threatens the heart is dissipated and dispelled. As is written in the *Qur'an,* "Then their skins and their hearts become gentle with the remembrance of God." (39:23)

The continuous practice of zekr causes the 'Lord of zekr' to dominate the kingdom of the heart, driving away whatever is not the thought of Him. Once the 'Lord of zekr' has taken up residence, the

40 heart grows attached and finds peace, to the extent that whatever is not Him will now be turned away. As the *Qur'an* states, "The hearts of those who believe are set at rest through God's remembrance; indeed, by God's remembrance (only) are hearts set at rest." (13:28)

In the words of Shaikh Majdoddin Baghdadi:

> *Inasmuch as the heart*
> > *is touched by the ways of the world,*
> *Is the hand stayed*
> > *from mastering the ways of the world.*
>
> *Once there was a heart*
> > *and a thousand different thoughts;*
> *Now there is naught*
> > *but* La ilaha illa'llah.

The *Mersadol-ebad* (*Ambush of the Travelers*) describes the above process in this manner:

> The king of Love sends down to the city of the heart his royal banner which is planted at the crossroads where the heart and spirit and body and soul meet. He has the royal constable of yearning capture and bind the wayward self with the rope of seeking, bringing it to the execution place of the heart. There, at the base of the royal banner of Love, its head of desire is severed with the sword of zekr and hung upon the tree of devotion.

As Rumi has written in the *Mathnawi:*

> *The howl of monsters has a familiar ring,*
> > *'Tis a call to oblivion that they sing.*
>
> *They cry, "Come hither! We'll give you a name."*
> > *They cajole the caravan, proffering fame.*
>
> *The monsters tempt man with artful seduction,*
> > *Leading him on to final destruction.*

It is just at the end that these monsters take shape
As the ravenous wolf and lion at the gate.

The monsters cry out, "Reputation!"
"Fatten your purse and cherish high station!"

Boring subtly within, they slyly insist;
Yet the secrets are opened to those who resist.

Remembrance of God can these voices banish;
In the inner eye's light will these vultures vanish.

Remembrance of a thing brings its qualities to existence,
As every accident needs an essence for subsistence.

In the *Mersadol-ebad,* the negative qualities dominating the self are symbolized as hoodlums and thugs, who, after surrendering and becoming slaves, respond in the words of the repentent Adam and Eve, "O Our Lord, we have wronged ourselves; if Thou forgive us not and have not mercy on us, we will surely be among the lost." (*Qur'an,* 7:23). According to the text, the king of Love absolves the delinquents of their misdoings and bestows the cloak of bondage upon them, raising them to the rank of chamberlains of the heart.

Only when the realm of the heart has been purified of the agitation of the self's negative qualities and the mirror of the heart polished of its rust does the heart deserve to be raised to the kingdom of the Beauty of Unity and freedom from need.

In the Prophet's words, knock at a door
and it will finally be opened to you.
Wait on the street of a friend
and you will finally see his face.
Dig all day in the earth
and eventually you will reach pure water.

Rumi

At this point, the king of Love accedes to the throne of the heart and the minister of reason stands at the gate. The city of the heart becomes resplendent with the radiance of certainty and devotion, sincerity and generosity, trust in God, and all the noblest virtues. The real King now arrives at the hidden chamber of the heart and the original Beloved reveals her true Beauty.

But Love is jealous and will not rest until even the noble courtiers, in their turn, are driven forth from the throne of the heart by the force of *La ilaha* ("There is nothing. . ."), for even these positive qualities represent a vestige of 'otherness' to be rejected.

Once this occurs, the heart has reached the truth that is rightfully its own, recovering its pre-eternal purity and becoming the castle of the royal *illa'llah* (". . .but God"). The King has emptied the heart of any 'otherness' and made it His own realm, as described in the *Qur'anic* passage (20:111), "And all faces shall be humbled before the Ever-Lasting and Self-Subsistent God." This is the state referred to in the Sacred Tradition, "Neither My earth nor My heaven can encompass Me, yet the heart of My adorer contains Me."

From this point on, the command of God dominates all the attributes and parts of the Perfected One in accordance with the *Qur'anic* passage (12:21), "And truly, God is predominate over His affairs." In other words, no attribute or part can dominate by its own will unless God so wills and commands. This is the meaning of the Sacred Tradition:

I become his ear, so he can listen with that ear.
I become his eye, so he can see with that eye.
I become his tongue, so he can speak with that tongue.
I become his hand, so he can grasp with that hand.
And I become his foot, so he can walk with that foot.

Here, the heart has finally become the abode for the manifestation of all God's Attributes.

So much He sat facing my open heart,
my heart was imbued with His nature and ways.

Even the mud when accompanied by flowers
acquires floral colors and fragrant aromas.

Maghrebi

THE DIFFERENT NAMES OF GOD AND THE GREATEST NAME

Some of the Names of God identify the Divine Essence, while others indicate the Divine Attributes. It is up to the master to decide which of these to inculcate, according to the disciple's capacity and spiritual state. It should be understood though that whenever one of the Divine Names is remembered, God is being remembered by all of His Names at once. As Shah Ni'matullah has said:

For all of God's Names the essence is One.
So all of the Names are in fact but One.

It should also be understood that the Greatest Name of God is actually like a kind of alchemy or 'Simurgh'.[2] In the words of Imam J'afar Sadeq, "Free your heart from all that is not the remembrance of God. Then call Him by whatever Name you wish, and that becomes the Greatest Name."

THE REPETITION OF ZEKRS

Some 'shaikhs of the Path' have prescribed a specific number of repetitions of each zekr. For example, the Name 'Allah' might be repeated sixty-six times because that is the sum of its letters when valued according to one numerological system.

Other shaikhs, however, have not considered the number of repetitions to be important. This is, in fact, correct since attention to the number of repetitions will only destroy the concentration and

2. See Attar's *Conference of the Birds* (ed.).

44   state of the sufi. Moreover, how can one forget the self—one of the conditions of zekr—while attending to the process of enumeration? In the words of Bayazid, "Zekr is measured not in number, but in intensity of presence."

THE STAGES OF ZEKR

There are various stages of zekr:

1.   Zekr is remembered with the tongue, but not felt in the heart. Some shaikhs have said that even when zekr is experienced only verbally, it has at least some effect.

2.   The heart, as well as the tongue, becomes involved in remembrance, but zekr has not yet become firmly established in the heart. Here, one should make an effort to pretend that zekr has taken root so that the heart will continue to be aroused by it. Without the pressure of such continued effort, the heart will go its own way and turn away from remembrance.

3.   Zekr comes to dominate the heart and becomes firmly rooted. Now, only great effort can detach the heart from its remembrance and involve it in the remembrance of anything else.

4.   *That which is remembered (God), rather than the remembrance, comes to dominate the heart. At this point, there is no question of whether the zekr should be in Arabic or Persian or English, for the words of the zekr are the concern only of the* nafs *(self). Here, the traveler, in complete involvement with the Beloved, forgets even the Name of God. This is the first step of sufism and the beginning of the 'passing away of the self in God' (fana) in which both the sufi and the remembrance have been forgotten!*

The sufi in this state says:

*So lost did I become from myself
through Your remembrance on the path,*

That now I ask for news about myself
from whoever I pass.

Sana'i, in the *Hadiqatol-haqiqah* (*Walled Garden of Truth*), has written:

> *Striving on the path is but remembrance of God,*
> *not hanging idly around the gatherings of the path.*

> *Though remembrance of the Beloved is your guide at first,*
> *you'll get to the point where it becomes a burden.*

> *The diver seeking for a way in the depths of the ocean*
> *is killed in the end by that same deep ocean.*

> *The dove being absent from God says, 'coo, coo'[3];*
> *if 'you' is still present, how can you shout 'Hu'[4]?*

> *Those in God's presence are content facing calamity;*
> *if you're not in God's presence, give vent to your shrieks.*

The stages of zekr have also been described in the following manner:

1. Zekr of the ordinary ones—the profit of which is to take the traveler away from negligence.

2. Zekr of the elect—in which the veil of reason and discernment is torn away from the rememberer, and with his whole heart he is attentive to God.

3. Zekr of the elect of the elect—which is the passing away of the rememberer in the One who is remembered.

---

3. 'Coo', in Persian, is a way of saying, "where is he?" (ed.).
4. *Hu:* one of the Names of God in Arabic, meaning 'He' (ed.).

46   Many other statements have been made about the stages of zekr. According to Shah Ni'matullah, while in the beginning the rememberer thinks *he* is remembering God, at the end he realizes that it is actually God who is remembering God and thus there is no longer any perception of zekr, for God is now both rememberer and remembrance.

Bayazid has described his experience thus, "Thirty years I spent in remembrance of God. When I stopped, I realized that my very zekr was my veil." Jonaid has stated, "Tasavvuf is first a remembrance, then an ecstasy, then neither one nor the other, until nothing remains as it truly never had been."

In the words of Abol-hasan Nuri, "The truth of zekr is the passing away of the *zaker* (rememberer) in the *Mazkur* (One who is remembered)."

Attar, in the *Tazkeratol-owliya* (*Tales of the Saints*), has recounted the following incident in the life of Jonaid:

It is said that on one occasion a disciple violated the ethic of Jonaid's order and therefore left the service of his master. He set out on a journey, traveling until he came upon another group of sufis. One day Jonaid passed by and saw him, whereupon the devotee was overcome with awe at the master's presence and fell down, cutting his head so that it bled profusely. Each drop of blood flowed in such a way as to form the Name 'Allah'. Jonaid, upon seeing this, reproached the devotee for making the claim that he had reached the state to which his remembrance aspired, saying that any child could come this far and that only a true man might reach the Remembered.

Rumi, in his account of the love of Zoleikha for Joseph, has written:

> *When Zoleikha sought to call out*
> *Joseph's name,*
> *'Incense', 'rue', and 'aloes'*
> *all meant the same.*

Within these names, his true name
  did she hide
Which but to intimates
  she did confide.

If a hundred thousand names she gathered
  in a heap,
She meant just 'Joseph' which in her heart
  she did keep.

In hunger, she would quote his name
  and be lifted up,
Thirsty, she would drink and swoon
  with nectar from that cup.

Joseph's name in ecstasy would quench
  her fervid thirst,
For by that heavenly mead was
  her state of rapture nursed.

The very instant that cherished name
  caused pain,
Straightforth the flush of comfort
  solace for her heart became.

Transcendent warmth against the cold,
  like a fleecy cover,
By love's name glowed
  upon the yearning lover.

Water round the fish provides
  its daily bread,
One element at once food and drink,
  dress and bed.

So is the lover like a child drinking milk
from the breast,
Knowing nought in the two worlds but that
out-flowing blessedness.

CONCLUSION

Zekr is the product of God's 'Loving-kindness' (*mohabbat*), the seed being the Loving-kindness implanted in the sufi's heart by God and the fruit being the sufi's remembrance of the Beloved. As the *Qur'an* (5:54) says, "He loves them, and they love Him." That is, God's Loving-kindness always precedes man's. Until God loves a devotee and remembers him, it will be difficult for the devotee to remember and love God.

Zekr also awakens intuition in the heart, enabling it to perceive the Divine Attributes and inspiring the sufi to love God. This familiarity with God brings about a lasting peace in the sufi's heart. "Indeed, by God's remembrance are hearts set at rest." (*Qur'an,* 13:28)

The truth of zekr, then, is that it is God who first remembers the disciple. Thus, some sufi mystics have interpreted the *Qur'anic* passage (29:45), "Verily, prayer restrains one from evil, and certainly the remembrance of God is greatest," to mean that while daily prayer is a remembrance performed by order of the *shari'at* to restrain one from misdoing, the greater remembrance is God's remembrance of man. In the same way, the inculcation of zekr by the 'master of the Path' is considered a kind of "greater remembrance".

In the words of the sufi mystic Ruzbehan:

Zekr is a light emanating from God's manifestation. By its purity, the hearts of sufis are drawn to the Beloved.

ور برانی و گرم بنده مخلص خوانی

روی برتافتن از حضرت سلطانی نیست

فكر

FEKR

The Sufi Way
of Contemplation

ONE WHO KNOWS GOD

Whoever knows God will be freed
    from the memory of what is other.
All who become a patient of He
    know that the pain of He is the cure.
Worship of self is not the worship of God;
    this truth is our explanation.
Be non-existent so you can truly be;
    know that the true, freed being is God.
The drop didn't see itself and so became the ocean;
    the former was extinction, the latter permanence.
No differences or disputes exist among the sober drunkards;
    whoever becomes a sober drunkard will be pure.
The light-giver* of all is one, One,
    though a thousand mirrors there may be.

*Nurbakhsh

O THE ONE WHO CANNOT BE REACHED THROUGH REASON

O brother, you are your very thought.
As for the rest, you are only hair and bone.
If your thought is a rose, you're a garden of roses.
If it's a thorn, you're but fuel for the stove.

Rumi

Fekr is defined in the dictionary as contemplation or reflection. The *Qur'an* has many passages emphasizing *fekr:*

. . .Verily in this matter there are signs for those who reflect. (This phrase comes at the end of many verses.)

We sent down to you this scripture that you might clarify to the people whatever descends to them so that they might reflect. (16:44)

There are those who remember God standing and sitting and reclining, and who reflect upon the creation of heaven and earth. (3:190)

Thus, God makes clear His signs to you that you might
reflect (upon them). (2:266)

Thus, We explain fully the signs for those who reflect.
(10:24)

So tell them parables that they might reflect. (7:176)

And we sent forth proverbs to the people that they might
reflect (upon them). (59:21)

And We sent amongst you love and compassion. Verily, in
this there are signs for those who reflect. (30:21)

Say, 'Are the blind and the seeing alike? Do you not then
reflect?' (6:50)

A number of Prophetic Traditions also speak about the practice
of fekr:

An hour's reflection is worth more than seventy years of worship.

Reflection causes the enlightenment of the heart.

There is no worship like reflection.

And in the words of 'Ali, "Awaken your heart with reflection."

FEKR FROM THE POINT OF VIEW OF THE 'AREF

An 'aref is one who strives to reach God by means of knowledge
and virtue. Whereas a philosopher draws two premises together with
his intellect in order to generate a conclusion, the 'aref draws two
kinds of knowledge together in his heart in order to reach a third and
different kind of knowledge. For the 'aref, this is the significance of
contemplation. As long as a third kind of knowledge is not acquired,
he considers himself to be involved only in recollection of previous
knowledge.

According to al-Ghazali in the *Kimia-ye Sa'adat* (*Alchemy of*

Happiness), contemplation brings about a succession of develop-
ments: first, an awareness (*ma'refat*); then, a quality (*halat*); and
finally an action (*'amal*).

FEKR FROM THE POINT OF VIEW OF THE SUFI

For sufis, the object of contemplation is the Absolute Beloved,
everything else being purged from the mind. Whereas the contemplation of the 'aref is done more with the intellect, the contemplation of
the sufi is more involved with Love. In other words, the
contemplation of the 'aref and that of the sufi are not the same.

In describing these two kinds of contemplation, it is useful to
consider the following definitions which various 'arefs and sufi
shaikhs, according to their different spiritual states, have given:

1. "The noblest and most worthy gathering is to sit in contemplation in the Garden of Unity." (Jonaid)

2. "Contemplation is the heart's grasping of the meaning of
objects for the sake of comprehending the Subject." (Jorjani)

3. "Contemplation is to be effaced in the remembrance of God."
(Shah Mohammad Darabi)

4. "The one who prays and fasts is near to people, while the one
who contemplates is near to God." (Shaikh Abu'l-hasan Kharaqani)

5. "Whosoever contemplates properly can neither speak nor act
without sincerity." (Abu-'amra Najid)

6. "Sitting in contemplation for one hour in the state of witnessing
is worth more than a thousand accepted pilgrimages." (Attar)

7. "Speech without wisdom is a plague, and silence without
contemplation is lust and negligence, and the noblest action is to
contemplate with self-negation." (Hasan Basri)

8. "Contemplation penetrates manifestations to perceive the work
of the Divine." (Hares Mohasebi)

9. "One hour in contemplation is worth more than a night of prayer." (Hasan Basri)

10. "The apostles asked Jesus if there was anyone like him on earth. 'Yes,' he replied, 'anyone whose speech is invocation, whose silence is contemplation, and whose perception is opened by awareness of the signs.' " (al-Ghazali)

11. "Thought for the ordinary man is plunging into the sea of illusion, while contemplation for the elect is being immersed in the ocean of understanding." (Ruzbehan)

12. "Contemplation brings you to God, while prayer brings you God's rewards. That which brings you to God has more value than that which brings you to something other than God." (Fakhr-e Razi)

13. "In the beginning, contemplation directs the attention towards the needed understanding, while at the end contemplation turns one from knowledge to inquiry, from form to meaning, and from the created to the Creator." (Shah Ni'matullah)

FEKR AS PRACTICED BY THE 'AREF

The practice of contemplation for the 'aref is carried out in two stages: upon the self and upon God.

1. Contemplation upon the self

Contemplation upon the self is referred to in the *Qur'anic* passage in which God says, "Do they not reflect upon themselves?" (30:8)

In this kind of contemplation, the 'aref undertakes a process of analyzing his weaknesses and negative qualities, both outward and inward, while at the same time striving to isolate and purge them. He also assesses his positive qualities and attempts to cultivate them so that they ornament his being. Hasan, the saint of Basra and disciple of

'Ali, taught that contemplation is a mirror which reflects a person's good and bad qualities.

For the 'aref, contemplation upon the self may also involve pondering from where and how he has come into existence, for what purpose he exists, and where he is going. Here, he reflects upon the *Qur'anic* passage (2:156), "Verily, it is from God we come and it is to God we shall return," and knows that he has come from God and will return to Him. Thus, he considers how he can go towards God and what he can do to please Him. He might also concentrate upon the meaning of the Sacred Tradition, "I was a hidden Treasure. I desired to be known, thus I created the world that it might know Me."

Day and night my only thought
is why I am ignorant of the states of my heart.
From whence have I come? and wherefore have I come?
where am I headed? will you not show me my home?
How rapturous the day I fly towards the Friend's abode,
beating my wings in hope of reaching that home.

Rumi

Still another object of contemplation for the 'aref may be the fact that everything other than the Truth is null and void, and that whatever is null and void cannot know the Truth. Similarly, he may reflect upon the fact that he is a part and God the Whole, and that the part cannot comprehend the Whole. Here, the 'aref attempts to relinquish all that is null and void in order to arrive at the Truth, endeavoring to leave the part and merge with the Whole in order to perceive in all parts the Whole through Its eye.

Reflection is passing from the false to the True,
Transcending the part to perceive the Whole.

Shabestari

In regard to contemplation upon the self, 'arefs have said, "Your contemplation upon yourself is sufficient for you (to know God)."

There are three kinds of contemplation upon God: contemplation upon the Essence, contemplation upon the Attributes, and contemplation upon the Effects.

a. Contemplation upon the Essence

Contemplation upon the Essence of God is impossible since the temporary cannot reflect upon the Eternal nor the illusory comprehend the Real. In the words of Shah Ni'matullah:

> *Since whatever is not God is null and void,*
> *how can such nothingness reach the Eternal?*

Al-Ghazali in the *Alchemy of Happiness* recounts that ibn 'Abbas, cousin and companion of the Prophet, once told Mohammad that some people were attempting to reflect upon the Essence of God. The Prophet replied that they should reflect upon the creations of God rather than upon God Himself, "for indeed," he added, "you do not have the capacity to reflect upon the Essence." As Sana'i has said:

> *The intellect can as easily reach*
> *His deepest Essence,*
> *As a piece of floating wreckage*
> *can reach to the depths of the sea.*

Mohammad also said, "Reflect upon everything except the Essence of God." And Imam Reza advised, "Whatever conception you have of a thing, conceive of God as independent of it."

> *The Prophet recommended that we refrain from making*
> *the Essence of God the subject of our reflection.*

> *Though you think contemplation upon His Essence is possible,*
> *in fact your view has with the Essence no connection.*

Since on the way towards God a hundred thousand veils exist,
to think you contemplate His Essence is only imagination.

Rumi

b. Contemplation upon the Attributes

Since the Attributes of God are the same as His Essence,
contemplation upon the truth of them is as difficult as contemplation
upon the Essence itself. However, it is possible to traverse the Divine
Attributes in the sense that the traveler, through continuous
remembrance of the various Names of the Attributes, exposes himself
to the Grace inherent in them. The individual will absorb this Grace
according to his capacity and potential. From some Names, he may
even be so filled that he becomes, to some extent, the manifestation of
the Attributes. That is, in accordance with the statement, "You
become qualified with the Qualities of God," the traveler here may
reach the state (*hal*) of 'having passed away in the Divine Attributes'.

c. Contemplation upon the Effects

The effects of God can be witnessed, and therefore contemplated,
both within the self and outside the self. In both instances, one is led
from the effect to the Cause, from the creation to the Creator, and
from the realm of the defined (limited existence) to the Undefined or
Unbounded (Absolute Existence).

Contemplation upon the effects of God, however, will have
results only if one is liberated from the desires of the self, for those
who are entangled in the demands of the self suffer from a kind of
illness and therefore contemplate in an unbalanced way.

Imam Mohammad Baqer advised his followers not to reflect
upon the Essence of God, but rather to reflect upon the grandeur of
the creation if they sought to contemplate God's Greatness.

In the words of Shaikh Shabestari:

Though contemplation on God's gifts is a condition of the path,
contemplation upon the Essence is only a transgression.

Contemplation upon the Essence is useless and vain,
for it is impossible to acquire what has already been gained.

Since all that exists is illuminated by God's Essence,
that which exists cannot illuminate the Essence.

As all the universe is by His Light manifested,
how can He be comprehended by that which is manifested.

The Light of the Essence cannot be contained by the signs,
for the Light of His Glory is triumphant over the signs.

When Jonaid was asked about contemplation, he replied that it had several aspects. Contemplation upon the Divine signs, he explained, leads to knowledge of God. Contemplation upon the Divine gifts brings about loving-kindness. Contemplation upon the attributes of the self and God's mercy towards the self produces shame in the individual. And contemplation upon the Divine admonishments, and punishments and rewards results in fear of God.

Jonaid added that if someone questions why contemplation upon the Divine admonishments produces fear of God, it should be explained that one who becomes involved in such contemplation will conclude that he is going to be punished for his past sins and therefore will give up his trust in God's generosity, leading him to commit further sins. By committing more and more sins, he will eventually be led to the fear of God. (cited in Attar's *Tazkeratol-owliya*)

At this point, it may be useful to consider contemplation as described by Khwajeh 'Abdollah Ansari. In his book, *Sad Meidan* (A *Hundred Fields of Battle*), Ansari has taught that contemplation grows out of the sphere of control (where the desires of the self are resisted). According to Ansari, the heart travels the path just as the self does, and contemplation for the heart is the impetus for such traveling.

Ansari has defined contemplation in the *Sad Meidan* as a process of putting together known data in order to arrive at the Unknown. He goes on to divide contemplation into three categories—the prohibited contemplation, the recommended contemplation, and the necessary contemplation.

1. There are three types of prohibited contemplation: contemplation upon the Divine Essence, which is the seed of bewilderment (since the Essence cannot be comprehended); contemplation upon the Divine rewards and punishments, which is the seed of reviling (since one will be unable to accept God's ways); and contemplation upon the secrets of creation, which is the seed of hostility (since one will be unable to decipher these secrets).

2. There are also three types of recommended contemplation: contemplation upon the creations of the Creator, which is the seed of wisdom; contemplation upon the variety of creation, which is the seed of insight; and contemplation upon God's gifts, which is the seed of loving-kindness.

3. The necessary contemplation, which is of primary importance, is upon one's own tasks. This consists of analyzing one's shortcomings in obedience to God and is the seed of shame. Contemplation here also involves reflecting upon one's duties and responsibilities in the future, this contemplation being the seed of fear.

Included in the necessary contemplation is the cultivation of a sense of 'spiritual supplication' (*niyaz*), the merit of which is to see God. Cultivating such a sense of supplication involves contemplation, reflection, and retrospection. The contemplation is upon deeds (how one should act), the reflection is upon discourse (what one should say), and the retrospection is upon forgiveness (how one should forgive). From such contemplation, one understands that one's deeds should be virtuous, one's discourse true, and one's forgiveness pure.

In another book, *Manazel-al Saerin* (*Stages of the Pilgrim*), Ansari has taught that contemplation is the seeking of insight so as to be able to better comprehend the Sought-for. In this instance, he has also divided contemplation into three categories:

1. Contemplation upon the Truth of the Divine Unity, which is merging with the ocean of self-negation and refutation (i.e. the state in which everything is Him and there is no longer any 'I' and 'you'). Liberation from this ocean of self-negation is impossible, Ansari has stated, except by the light of discovery and appeal to knowledge.

2. Contemplation upon the subtle intricacies of the creation, which is the water that slakes the thirst of wisdom.

3. Contemplation upon the meaning of one's actions and states, which makes traveling on the path easier.

Ansari has elaborated upon these three types of contemplation by stating that release from the first can occur through knowledge of the limitations of reason, discouragement in attaining the Unattainable End, and grasping the rope of the exaltation of God.

The subtle intricacies of the creation, which are the object of the second type of contemplation, can be comprehended by acceptance with contentment of whatever God brings, receptiveness to the Divine Will, and liberation from the bonds of desire.

The third kind of contemplation, upon the meaning of one's actions and states, can be accomplished by the pursuit of knowledge, detachment from social customs, and awareness of those moments when one is involved in what is not God.

FEKR IN SUFI PRACTICE

Contemplation for the sufi is the traversing of the Path in the heart, born through the remembrance of God. By the remembrance of God, the lightning of the Divine manifestations comes to illuminate the house of the heart. With this illumination, the heart's contemplation becomes awakened and is transformed into a guide on the Path of Truth.

While 'rational' contemplation is woven, 'heart-based' contemplation is to be found. In rational contemplation the motivation and guiding force is reason, whereas in heart-based contemplation the motivation and master is God.

> *Give up your reason and be with the One,*
> *for a bat cannot bear the light of the sun.*
> *Wherever the Light of God is the guide,*
> *what need is there for Gabriel's advice?*
>
> *Shabestari*

Three kinds of heart-based contemplation can be enumerated:

1. Contemplation in the State of Seeking

For the person who is in a state of seeking but has not yet found a master and begun to travel the Spiritual Path (*tariqat*), contemplation begins when God creates in his (or her) heart the thought of finding a spiritual guide. By means of this contemplation, a state of restlessness is created in him that does not cease until he has found what has been lost. This can occur, however, only if he receives the grace of partaking from the banquet of Love.

> *Contemplation should occur in such a fashion*
> *as to open the path and bring forth a king.*
> *Consider that one a king who is free from his kingship*
> *though his radiance lights up the moon and the sun.*
>
> *Rumi*

2. Contemplation for the Initiate

For the beginner on the Spiritual Path, one whose languid thought has not yet been kindled by the warmth of remembrance, contemplation is the revelation in the heart of the master's spiritual beauty by means of illumination. Hence, some masters of the Path have said that contemplation is the manifestation of the spiritual face of the master.

3. Contemplation for the Advanced Sufi

From the warmth of remembrance, the languid thought of the sufi is gradually stirred to life and his spirit (*ruh*) grows familiar with the Hidden. Some sufi mystics have said that contemplation is the journeying of the heart through the spheres of the Hidden. According to Zo'n-nun of Egypt, "Whoever contemplates with his heart has the Hidden revealed to his spirit."

Thus, contemplation for the advanced sufi results from his remembrance and becomes his guide on the Path. In the words of Attar:

Contemplation is the traveler's guide on the path,
a guide acquired through constant remembrance.

Remembrance is what brings forth contemplation, which then
brings forth a hundred thousand hidden meanings.

Rational contemplation is fine for discourse,
but the heart's contemplation is for one of action.

Though contemplation be for only an hour,
yet it is better than seventy years of prayer.

Or in the words of Rumi:

So much we've said, you reflect upon the rest;
if that doesn't work, then turn to zekr.

Remembrance is what arouses the heart's contemplation, so make it a sun for your languid reflection.*

Though the principle of the matter is Divine attraction,
O sufi, don't depend upon that and neglect your duties.

Since relinquishing such duties is only arrogance,
how can you compare that to losing your existence?

Concerning this true contemplation, Shaikh Abu'l-hasan Kharaqani has said:

God bestowed upon me a contemplation, such that I perceived in it everything that He has created. I became totally immersed in this contemplation. It became my preoccupation night and day until it opened the eye of my heart and became harshness, loving-kindness, fear, and heaviness.

From that contemplation, I became plunged into the Divine Unity and reached the point where contemplation was transformed into wisdom, guidance upon the direct path, and kindness for the whole of creation. I could find no one kinder than myself among all of His creations. I wished to die instead of all of the creations so that death would never be encountered again. I wished Him to judge me instead of all the creations so that none would be judged on the Day of Judgement. And I wished to reap all of the retribution meted out to mankind so that no one would ever have to experience hell.

About this same kind of contemplation, Rumi has written:

Your thought is only the form,
His thought is the spirit within it.
Your currency is only paper,
but His has gold behind it.

And in the words of Hafez:

Thought and opinion have no place
in the world of the true sufis;
For to be self-centered and opinionated
is a transgression on our way.

In the circle of destiny,
we are but a dot made by the compass.
Your contemplation is our grace,
and Your command our reference.

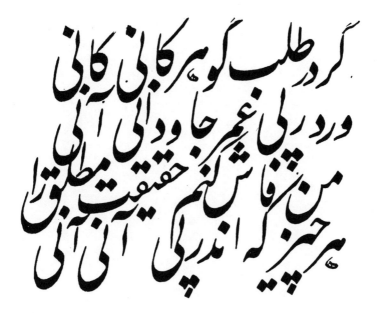

گر در طلب گوهر کانی کانی
ور در ره منزلی نغمی جاودانی آنی
من فاش کنم حقیقت مطلق را
هر چیز که اندر پی آنی آنی

مراقبه

MORAQEBEH

The Sufi Way
of Meditation

LOVE'S LAW

If a mystic makes a claim that comes from the mind,
in Love's law that claim is false.

Perfection draws imperfection toward itself;
he who is not upset by imperfection, in truth
is perfect.

The seeker of the shore didn't become drowned in the
Ocean of Love,
for one who is seeking the shore is not a lover.

Although in the way of the lover there is none
but the Beloved,
sobriety, passion, rapture, and the extinction of the
self and its qualities are also involved.

The light of union blinds the eye that discriminates forms,
yet he who thinks he is in union with the Beloved
has lost true discrimination.

The wine drinkers are selfless and drunken, and the winegiver
is present;
here, whoever seems sober is lazy.

O Nurbakhsh, our days have been spent in wine worship
since we learned that life without wine is worthless.

IN THE NAME OF THE SUPREME GUARDIAN

I was drawn to the Beloved
Like a moth to a flame;
When I came to my senses,
I was burned up in the flame.

Asheq-e Esfahani

Moraqebeh is two people taking care of and protecting each other. The sages of the Path have said about *moraqebeh* that just as God takes care of and protects man, so man in his heart must take care of and protect God.

Mohiyeddin ibn 'Arabi has written:

Meditate upon God in all situations,
for God meditates upon you.

As said in the *Qur'an*, "Verily, God watches over you. . ." (4:1) and "God watches over all things." (33:52)

> *Moraqebeh is keeping oneself away from what is not God, both outwardly and inwardly, and concentrating one's whole being upon God.*

Sufi masters have given many definitions of moraqebeh, such as:

Moraqebeh is being inwardly pure towards God, both when alone and with people.
(Ebrahim al-Khavvas)

Moraqebeh is relinquishing the control and will of the self, followed by the expectation of His Grace and Will, and turning away from whatever is not Him.
(Kashshaf, *Estelahat-e fonun*)

Moraqebeh is the presence of the heart with God and the absence of the heart from all that is other than God.
(*Ghiyaso'l-loghat*)

Moraqebeh is the protection of one's being from all that is not Divine and the concentration of one's attention upon God.
(The *Estelahat* of Abdo'l-Razzaq-e Kashani)

Moraqebeh is the observance of the secrets with regard to God.
(*Asraro'l-fateheh*)

In the words of Shaikh Ruzbehan, "Moraqebeh is the involvement of the spirit (*ruh*) in God's Breath." This statement refers to the Prophetic Tradition which declares, "Verily, the Lord has provided Breath in all your days; put yourself in its way." (*Ehya'ol-'olum*)
As Rumi has written:

these days is coming forth;
So keep your inner ear aware
and steal this Breath away."

Among you came a Breath, then it passed,
bestowing on whoever it wished a soul.
Another Breath will soon come forth,
O sufi, keep watchful, or you'll miss this too.

THE KINDS OF MORAQEBEH

Moraqebeh is in two directions: from God to the creation, and from the creation to God.

1. From God to the Creation

a. The Divine Moraqebeh towards the Whole of Creation

The world of substances exists only insofar as it is sustained through accidents. Whenever an accident through which a substance subsists fades away, that substance will also cease to subsist. Since each accident will finally cease to exist at one time or another, God must continually watch over the heavenly and earthly substances so that when one particular accident perishes, a similar or contrasting accident is created by Him, thus preserving the existence of those substances. This is the meaning of the *Qur'anic* passage, "At every moment He is involved with creation." (55:29)

Shaikh Ruzbehan has said:

Moraqebeh is God's awareness over every particle of the creation from the Divine Throne to the lowest phenomenon, and His overseeing of all the Attributes for the purpose of granting them grace.

b. The Divine Moraqebeh which evokes Religious Action

By God's attention upon them, His devotees are stirred to perform the actions sanctioned by the *shari'at* and to refrain from those that are prohibited.

c. The Divine Moraqebeh towards the Elect

Here, God pays attention to His friends in order to see what they do for Him. This moraqebeh is described in the *Qur'anic* passage, "Verily, God has purchased from the faithful their selves and their goods." (9:111)

> *God is my customer, He takes me up*
> *for only He can purchase.*
>
> *Rumi*

The moraqebeh of the elect is known only to God, for according to a Sacred Tradition, "My saints are under my shelter, no one knows them but Me." These friends of God are satisfied and made content from this moraqebeh, as described in the *Qur'anic* verse, "Be aware, the friends of God have no fear and do not sorrow." (10:62)

2. From the Creation to God

a. The Moraqebeh of the Shari'at

The moraqebeh of the *shari'at* is the result of attention to God's utterance (*Qur'an,* 96:14), "Does he not know that God sees him?" In this moraqebeh, man knows that God is aware of what he does. Thus, he is watchful for God watches him. Ansari has told the following story in this regard:

> Ibn 'Omar happened upon a slave taking a flock of sheep to pasture. He said, "O slave, sell me one of these sheep." The slave replied that the sheep did not belong to him. Ibn 'Omar then said, "If the owner asks, tell him that a wolf has eaten it." The slave asked, "Where then is God?" Ibn

'Omar was so pleased with this reply that he bought the 75
slave and sheep from the owner and set the man free, giving
him the sheep for his own.

One who practices this kind of moraqebeh should be watchful
over both his thoughts and his actions. In the *Kimia-ye Sa'adat*
(*Alchemy of Happiness*), al-Ghazali has written:

> In the moraqebeh of thought, one should make an effort to
> maintain those thoughts that are from God and to
> relinquish those that are from the self. In the moraqebeh of
> action, one should be watchful over all of one's conduct—
> whether that conduct is obedient, sinful, or neither one nor
> the other. That is, with obedient conduct, one should
> endeavor to act with devotion and presence of heart. With
> sinful acts, one should feel shame and strive to refrain from
> such acts. And with actions that are neither sinful nor
> obedient, one should attempt to be polite and see the Giver
> in the Divine Gifts, knowing that one is always in His
> Presence.

Khwajeh 'Abdollah Ansari has called the moraqebeh of the
shari'at, "the moraqebeh of service", and said that it is the result of
three things:

1. Obedience to the Divine Commands.

2. Knowledge of the Sacred Traditions and Customs.

3. Awareness of one's hypocrisy.

In the words of Rumi:

> *Each moment you'll see the results of your work*
> *if you're watchful and manage to stay alert.*

If you've grasped the rope of being vigilant,
your yearning won't last to the Day of Judgement.
Be watchful if you want to achieve a heart,
for after each action something will be acquired.
If your striving is even greater than this,
you'll rise yet higher than moraqebeh.

b. The Moraqebeh of Faith

The moraqebeh of faith is the result of being surrendered to God, as described in the *Qur'anic* passage (41:53), "Soon We will show them Our signs in the world and in their selves." A person involved in such moraqebeh observes God's signs both in the outside world and the world of selves, and sees God as the Doer in everything.

A man once asked ibn Mobarak to advise him. The answer he received was, "Watch for God." The man then asked for the interpretation of this statement and was told, "Always be in a state as if you were seeing God."

Ansari has called this moraqebeh, "the moraqebeh of time", and said that it can be attained through three things:

1. Annihilation of all desires.
2. Purification of all thoughts.
3. Predominance of kindness.

c. The Divine Moraqebeh

The Divine Moraqebeh is reserved for the saints of God, who see Him both inwardly and outwardly, in both solitude and society, and who say, "I see nothing unless I have seen God first."

Ansari has called this moraqebeh, "the moraqebeh of the secrets", stating that it too can be reached through three things:

1. Being lost to the world.
2. Abandoning the self.
3. Being filled with closeness to God.

This moraqebeh has also been called the moraqebeh of the sincere ones. The hearts of such beings are drowned in God, and their attention never strays to anything other than God. Sometimes, they are so drowned in God that if you talk to them they don't hear, and if you stand before them they don't see. 'Abdollah ibn Zeid was once asked if he knew anyone who was truly absorbed in the Creator rather than the creation. In answer, he addressed 'Ebato'l-Gholam who had just arrived. "Who did you see on the way coming here?" 'Ebato'l-Gholam replied, "No one." Ibn Zeid then explained that the man's way had been through the crowded bazaar.

To summarize then, there are two kinds of moraqebeh for sufis: the outward moraqebeh and the inward moraqebeh.

The outward moraqebeh involves the attention of the part (i.e. the individual) towards the Whole (i.e. God). The sufi in this state sees God in everything. Whatever he does is for Him, and whatever befalls him he knows to have come from Him.

The inward moraqebeh involves the attention of the Whole towards the Whole. Here, the sufi closes the eye that sees only fragments of Reality and opens the vision of the total Reality, in which the Divine meditates upon the Divine.

This is the ultimate moraqebeh for sufis, the only true meditation—the conditions of which will now be described.

THE CONDITIONS OF MEDITATION

The place where moraqebeh occurs should:

1. Be empty of everything other than God (that is, it should be a secluded place).

2. Preferably be on the ground floor of a building so that the arrival and departure of other people won't cause one to turn away from the state of meditation.

3. Be quiet.

78   4. Be clean.

5. Be soft and comfortable so that one's attention won't be distracted from God to oneself. (In the past, sufi masters have used sheep-skins for this purpose.)

6. Be free of any kind of odor so that one's sense of smell will remain unaffected.

THE RULES AND MANNERS (ADAB) OF MEDITATION

In meditation, the sufi should:

1. Have performed ablution (*wozu*).

2. Wear soft and light clothes, with buttons undone so as to keep the body completely relaxed.

3. Sit on the floor or ground.

4. Keep the body free from motion. (Shebli once saw Nuri meditating in such a state of stillness that even the hair of his body was motionless. He asked Nuri from whom he had learned such meditation. Nuri replied, "From a cat I saw sitting at a mousehole. In waiting for the mouse, he was even more still than I am now.")

5. Keep the eyes shut.

6. Close the window of thought and imagination, and forget everything but God—especially when starting to meditate.

7. Concentrate upon God and witness the printing on the heart. (In this, it is necessary to be instructed orally by the master or shaikh.)

8. Lose any sense of individual will—to the extent of forgetting even one's identity as the meditator.

9. Abandon all desire. (In the state of meditation, various desires, wishes, and fantasies will appear in the sufi's memory and thought, causing him to be distracted from the direct path. Therefore, these obstacles must be demolished. To accomplish this, there are special orders which have been handed down by the masters of the Path and which must be received orally from the master or shaikh.)

10. Face the *Qiblah,* the direction of Islamic prayer. (Although it is certainly correct as stated in the *Qur'an* (2:115) that ". . .wherever you turn, you find the face of God," by facing the *Qiblah* the meditator's outward attention is directed towards the outer Ka'ba— the House of God in Mecca, and thus is in harmony with his inward attention which should be directed towards the inner Ka'ba—namely, the heart or Throne of God.)

11. Develop the habit of meditating at least fifteen minutes in each 24-hour cycle, preferably during the hours of darkness.

THE POSITIONS OF MEDITATION

The sufi has the alternative of three positions of meditation:

1. Sitting erect on the knees with the legs folded under, placing the palm of the right hand on the left thigh and grasping the right wrist with the left hand. (Fig. 1)
   In this manner, the legs together form the Arabic word 'la' (U) which means 'no' or 'not'. The arms also form the same word, written ﯼ . As previously stated in the chapter *Zekr,* this position stresses the sufi's nothingness and the negation of his sense of 'I-ness'.

2. Sitting in the same way as figure one, except with the legs crossed. Here, both the arms and legs form the word 'la' in this way: ﯼ . (Fig. 2)

3. Sitting cross-legged, with knees raised and arms folded around the legs, left hand grasping the right wrist and head bowed slightly towards the heart. (Fig. 3)   In this position, the same 'la' shape is

formed. In the past, sufis often tied a *reshteh* (a belt made of a warp of threads loosely tied together at intervals) around the legs in order to maintain this position for a long period of time without tiring.

For extended periods of meditation the sufi may assume position #3 and rest his head, at the left eyebrow, on his left knee. (Fig. 4) Sa'di, in the *Golestan,* tells the story of a sufi meditating in this position who became totally drowned in the ocean of discovery. When the sufi returned from this state, a companion asked him what gift he had brought back to his brethren from the garden. The sufi replied, "I had in my mind that when I reached a rosebush, I would fill up the skirt of my robe with roses. But when I finally approached the rosebush, I became so drunk with the aroma of the roses that I lost my hold on my garment."

In the case of physical disability, the meditator may sit on a chair with his legs bent and parallel, head held upright, and hands in the same position as figure one. (Fig. 5)

THE BENEFIT OF MEDITATION FOR THE INITIATE

In the early stages of the Path, meditation provides a way of practicing self-control. After a great deal of effort, it leads to the point where one's restless thought becomes restrained and one's heart attains calmness and serenity, accompanied by closeness to God. Certainly, for one who lacks self-control, meditation will initially be difficult. But gradually, through the attention and assistance of the master, this difficulty will be dissolved.

For the beginner then, the result of success in meditation is the development of self-control, leading to the attainment of a 'unity of attention' to God.

THE BENEFIT OF MEDITATION FOR ADVANCED SUFIS

Meditation is one of the basic conditions for the attainment of voluntary death which is the aim of the *tariqat* or Spiritual Path. When the sufi arrives at peace-of-heart and closeness to God, he becomes the possessor of the *nafs-e motma'eneh*('self-at-rest'). To the

Divine Call, "O Self-at-Rest," he now replies by involvement in the
meditation of ". . .return to your Lord, well-pleased (with Him), (and)
He well-pleased with thee." (*Qur'an,* 89:28) Shah Ni'matullah has
said:

> The sufi in this state (*hal*) concentrates upon the Divine
> Gifts for the sake of receiving the gracious Breaths of
> Absolute Being. He turns away from whatever is not God
> and becomes drowned like us in the Ocean of Loving-
> kindness. He longs to see the Beloved, as foretold in the
> Sacred Traditions, "Know you that the yearning of the
> saints to see Me is long" and "Verily, My longing for them
> is still stronger." His heart and spirit (*ruh*), rather than
> his flesh and blood, hasten day and night to be in the Divine
> Presence, and his spirit longs to receive eternal life from
> Him.

Thus, as a result of such meditation, the sufi gradually becomes
estranged from the world of 'I' and 'you'. He loses even the sense of
meditation with its lingering quality of duality, God causing him to die
to himself and bringing him to life in Himself.

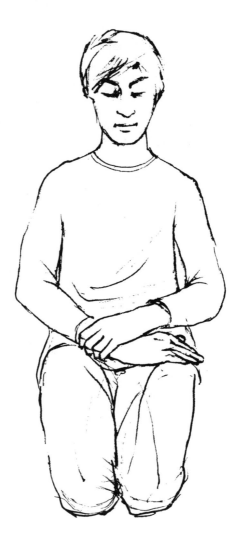

FIGURE 1

FIGURE 2

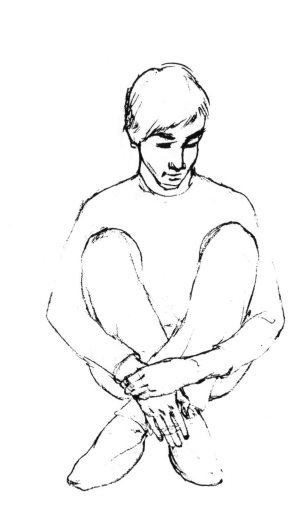

FIGURE 3

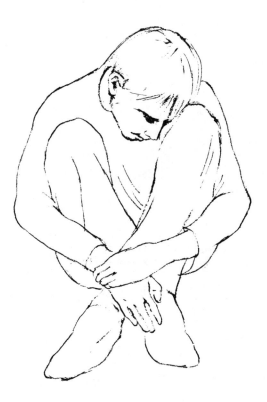

FIGURE 4

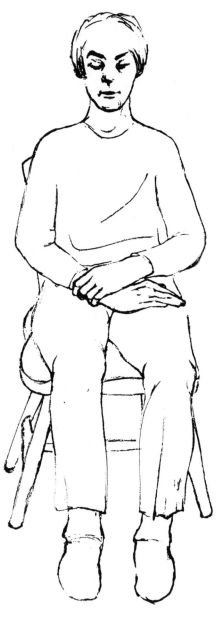

FIGURE 5

قُلِ اللّهُمَّ مَالِكَ الْمُلْكِ تُؤْتِي الْمُلْكَ مَن تَشَاءُ وَتَنزِعُ الْمُلْكَ مِمَّن تَشَاءُ وَتُعِزُّ مَن تَشَاءُ وَتُذِلُّ مَن تَشَاءُ بِيَدِكَ الْخَيْرُ إِنَّكَ عَلَىٰ كُلِّ شَيْءٍ قَدِيرٌ

محاسبه

MOHASEBEH

The Sufi Way of
Self-Examination

THE IMAGE OF EXISTENCE

Come, so we can wash away the image of existence
    and no longer speak of 'I' and 'we'.
Come, and like us let your thoughts pass away;
    forget both worlds and be silent.
Come, but beware of the shame of knowing;
    send those endless lines of learning from your head.
Come, so we can cast far away all sayable things
    and blind our eyes to all there is to see.
Come, we will be strangers to all
    and seem mad in the eyes of intellectuals.
Come, we'll empty ourselves of self
    and leave behind the disgrace of 'I'.
Come, and welcome unfulfillment,
    for we do not suppose our self's desires to be the goal.
Come, and be drowned in the Ocean of Unity,
    free from all thoughts of union and separation.
As this world is not even worth a grain of sand,
    other than what is old and new, it is nothing.

IN THE NAME OF THE SUPREME RECKONER

We cannot pick dates from the thistles that we grew,
and we cannot get silk from the wool that we wove.
We drew no line of contrition through our sins in the ledger,
and we inscribed no merits beside our capital transgressions.

Sa'di

As defined in the dictionary, *mohasebeh* means to balance accounts or to be precise in calculating. In sufi terminology, the meaning of *mohasebeh* is to take account of one's actions and thoughts in traveling towards God and to know that God always keeps a record of what one does.

The *Qur'an* has many passages which indicate that God keeps account of one's actions:

And verily, whether you manifest what is within you or keep it hidden, God will call you to account for it. (2:284)

Be aware! His is the Judgment, and He is the swiftest Reckoner. (6:62)

Their Lord metes out their reward, for God is swift in reckoning. (3:198)

91

Be in awe of God; verily, God is swift in reckoning. (5:4)

They receive retribution to the extent that they deserve, for God is a swift Reckoner. (14:51)

And for those who disbelieve, their actions are like mirages on the plain; in their thirst they reckon that they are reaching water, but they find nothing except God and His Reckoning; and God is a swift Reckoner. (24:39)

Verily, it is for you to inform and for Us to call to account. (13:40)

The following *Qur'anic* passage explicitly describes mohasebeh:

O you who believe, be aware of God and look well into yourselves to see what you have in stock for tommorrow. (59:18)

In the words of the Prophet of Islam:

Take account of your actions before God takes account of you, and weigh yourself before you are weighed, and die before you die. (cited in the Hadith collection, *Al-menhajo'l-qawi*).

SAYINGS OF THE GREAT SUFIS ABOUT MOHASEBEH

1. Abu-'Osman Maghrebi has said, "The noblest action on this Path is the examination of the self and the performance of one's duties with knowledge." (cited by Attar in the *Tazkeratol-owliya/ Tales of the Saints*)

2. Al-Ghazali, in the *Kimia-ye Sa'adat* (*Alchemy of Happiness*), has written:

Just before going to sleep each night, the devotee should take account of what his *nafs* (self) has done during the day, so that his profits and losses get separated from his investments. The investments here are the necessary actions; the profits are the recommended actions; and the losses are those actions which have been prohibited.

Just as one would purchase with care from a wily merchant, so must one bargain with caution in dealing with the self—for the self is a tricky and deceitful imposter that has a way of presenting its purposes in the garb of spiritual obedience so that one considers as profit what was really loss. In fact, in every action which is questionable, the devotee should examine his motivation carefully. If it is determined that the motivation came from the self, then compensation should be demanded of it.

3. In the *Sad Meidan* (*A Hundred Fields of Battle*), Ansari has written:

> The eleventh field of battle is mohasebeh. It develops out of the field of purification and has three foundations:
>
> a. Eliminating vicious deeds from one's dealings.
> b. Balancing Divine gifts with devoted service.
> c. Separating one's portion (i.e. that which is achieved through striving) from His portion (i.e. that which is granted by God).
>
> The way of achieving the first foundation is to know that all actions in which the self is involved and which are contrary to the *shari'at* are vicious and destructive.
>
> The way of achieving the second foundation is to know that one's unawareness of receiving Divine gifts is due solely to one's shortcomings and that for all the Divine gifts of which one is aware but ungrateful, compensation must be given. It is also to know that the misuse of Divine gifts will lead only to the destruction of one's belief.
>
> Achieving the third foundation involves knowing that service performed to gain something in this world is one's own concern, that service performed to gain something in the world hereafter is one's obligation, while service performed to reach God is one's price (i.e. God determines one's spiritual worth by the degree of one's service to Him).

94 4. In the *Mashrabo'l-arvah,* Ruzbehan has stated that mohasebeh
is the intellect's enumeration of one's inner transgressions and
thoughts of what is not God and its blaming of the 'commanding
self' (*nafs-e ammareh*) for following its own desires. In this station of
attending to religion, the intellect is a protector of the spirit (*ruh*).

Ruzbehan goes on to quote one mystic as saying that mohasebeh
is striving unceasingly to discipline the self so as to transform it. The
mystic adds that once the station of the mohasebeh is reached,
moraqebeh (meditation) becomes purified and the beauty of the *adab*
('rules and manners') of being in solitude and performing devotional
observances becomes illuminated. According to this mystic, the
essence of mohasebeh is that the angelic forces of the universe present
to the spirit (*ruh*) the transgressions that have been committed by the
self (*nafs*).

5. Suhravardi, in describing the process by which a particular state
(*hal*) is sometimes transformed into a station (*maqham*), has also
spoken of mohasebeh. In the *'Avarefo'l-ma'aref,* he has explained
that while the motivation for mohasebeh is originally awakened in
the inner being of the devotee, this motivation fades as the attributes
of the self reassert their dominance. It then returns, only to fade once
again.

In other words, due to the manifestation of the attributes of the
self, the devotee's state keeps vacillating until he finally receives
Divine assistance and the state of mohasebeh becomes dominant.
Here, the self is subdued and mohasebeh takes over the devotee's
free-will. Mohasebeh is now his sole abode, having become his
station rather than state. Thus, the state of mohasebeh is
transformed into the station of mohasebeh.

Once the devotee resides in the station of mohasebeh, the state of
moraqebeh becomes awakened. This state also rises and fades in
him, however, as negligence and error from time to time come to exist
in his inner being. Only when such negligence and error are dispelled
through Divine assistance does moraqebeh become a station.

In the first instance, the station of mohasebeh does not become
firmly settled in the devotee until the state of moraqebeh begins to
descend upon him. Similarly, the station of moraqebeh does not
become firmly settled in the devotee until the state of *moshahedeh*
(witnessing) begins to be manifested. When this state of witnessing
occurs, moraqebeh becomes a station.

6. Mohammad ibn-e Mahmud Amoli, in the *Nafayeso'l-fonun*, has written:

Mohasebeh means to be constantly searching into and examining the states and actions of the self. Day by day and hour by hour, one should take account of whatever arises in one's being, whether positive or negative, so as to become aware of the qualities of one's states.

Amoli adds that mohasebeh is regarded as the third of the traveler's stations on the Path.

* * *

In the early period of Islam, there existed a sufi order known as the Mohasebiyeh, which was founded by Hares Mohasebi (b.Basra —781, d.Baghdad—857 A.D.), a contemporary of Ahmad ibn-e Hanbal (the founder of the Hanbali school of Islamic Law).

In the *Tazkeratol-owliya*, Attar has written that Hares was given the title of Mohasebi because of his rigorous and assiduous devotion to the practice of mohasebeh. According to Attar, Hares has said:

Those who truly practice mohasebeh possess certain characteristics which become manifested in their speech and action. Through God's grace, such people reach the higher stations of the Path by means of their practice of mohasebeh. This can take place, however, only by having a strong will and rejecting the desires of the self. For one who acquires a strong will, opposition to the desires of the self will be easy. Thus, it is essential to develop one's will and to nurture the following characteristics which are known to bear fruit:

1. Never swearing in the Name of God, whether accidentally or deliberately, rightly or wrongly.

2. Never lying.

3. Never breaking a promise if at all feasible, while avoiding making promises as much as possible.

4. Never cursing another person (asking God to bring calamity upon that person), even one who has done harm.

5. Never intending ill towards other people (whether in word or deed) or praying for them to be punished, but rather tolerating everyone and everything for the sake of God.

6. Never accusing another person of infidelity, polytheism (*shirk*), or the causing of discord—for accusing anyone of such acts is farther from having grace upon people and closer to the Divine Wrath than refraining from such accusations.

7. Never having the intention to commit sins, either outwardly or inwardly (that is, dissociating one's whole being from everything that is not God).

8. Never putting the burden of one's pain or suffering on anyone else's shoulders, whether or not one's personal need is involved.

9. Never having any greed whatsoever for any of the creations, nor envying the possessions of others.

10. Never considering oneself higher than any other human being—for in this way one will arrive at nearness to God both in this world and the world hereafter, thereby attaining a high spiritual station and the perfection of honor.

THE KINDS OF MOHASEBEH

1. Mohasebeh-ye nafsi (of the self)

Each night before sleeping, the sufi should take a few minutes to examine his *nafs* (self) and enumerate all the positive and negative

actions he has done during the day. If he finds that his negative acts 97
have outnumbered his positive ones, he should resolve to compensate
for this imbalance the following day. If his positive acts have been
more numerous, he should not only avoid any sense of pride, but
resolve to redouble his efforts at eliminating all negative acts the next
day. In the event that his positive and negative acts are balanced, he
should endeavor to add to his positive ones.

The sufi should also take account of his thoughts in this kind of
mohasebeh. He should weigh his positive and negative thoughts
carefully, gradually emptying his mind of the negative ones and
replacing them with positive ones, for God punishes sufis even for
their negative thoughts.

Jonaid has told the following story in this regard:

I was once sitting outside the Shunizieh Mosque in
Baghdad waiting for a funeral ceremony to take place. All
the people of Baghdad were there to pray for the dead man.
Among them, I saw a poor man begging with a pious look. I
thought to myself, "If only this beggar worked in order to
provide for himself, it would be better."

When I returned home that evening and went about my
customary observances, I found it difficult to perform my
prayers and invocations. Because of this unaccustomed
difficulty, I was forced to remain awake until late at night.
Suddenly, I fell asleep. In a dream I saw the beggar being
brought to me at a banquet table and I was told to eat of his
flesh since I had gossiped behind his back.[1]

I replied that I had not gossiped behind his back, but
only thought something to myself. The answer I received
was, "You are not like ordinary people. From you even
such thoughts cannot be accepted, and therefore you must
ask for forgiveness from this man."

The next morning I searched for the man but couldn't
find him anywhere. Finally, I came upon him by a stream
where chives were being washed. He was sitting at the edge

1. A reference to the *Qur'anic* verse which says, "O you who believe, refrain from being too
free in your suspicions, for some suspicions are sinful; and do not meddle in other people's affairs or
gossip about others. Would any of you care to eat the flesh of his dead brother? Surely you would
not; fear God then. Verily, God is forgiving (to the repentent) and the Most Merciful." (49:12)

of the stream catching the stray greens which slipped through the washers' fingers and floated downstream.

I greeted him and went to speak, but he interrupted me, saying, "O Abo'l Qasem, are you going to think such thoughts again?" I told him no, and he replied, "May God forgive us both." (cited in the *Tarjomeh Resaleh Goshei - riyeh*)

2. Mohasebeh-ye tariqati (of the Path)

The condition of the 'mohasebeh of the Path' is that the sufi take account of his states, striving as much as possible to decrease his states of multiplicity and increase his state of Unity. In this way, he will advance each day towards the Divine Reality, coming ever closer to God. Here, he should remember the Tradition of the Prophet which states, "He whose days are equal is one who has lost."

The sufi climbs a ladder at the top of which is God. He should not count the rungs he has climbed, but rather take account of the way he has yet to travel.

The sufi should always be cognizant of the contracts he has with God and of his commitments to the master, and refrain from breaking these promises. He should be aware of the constant presence of the master and should never make any move contrary to the orders of the Path.

With each step that the sufi makes, he should take account of God, knowing that all his movements are for the sake of Him. Just as every breath he takes is in remembrance of God, every movement he makes is for the sake of God.

Finally, the sufi, having surrendered himself completely to God, should consider whatever comes to him as descended from the Divine and therefore good.

3. Mohasebeh-ye haqqi (of the Divine)

The shaikh of the Path should adapt his outer and inner being to the different kinds of states and stations that he has. For example, when in the state of being in contact with the creations (i.e. with others), he should be careful not to fall into self-worship. When in the station of being in contact with the Creator, he should refrain from speaking of his existence.

The claims of the shaikh should always be appropriate to his situation. Moreover, whatever he claims to be, he should in fact be. In this kind of mohasebeh, the shaikh should take account of his responsibilities not only to God on the one hand but to his disciples on the other. In the station of Unity, he should not speak of 'I' and 'you' or of his spiritual discoveries and abilities. In the realm of purification and loving-kindness, he should never be harsh or severe. And in the station of guiding, he should be careful not to become a veil between the disciple and God.

One who claims to be a 'master of the Path' should step upon both this world and the world hereafter rather than be greedy for the wealth of the world. The Perfected One is a stranger to whatever is not God; he is not the aquaintance of the possessors of wealth or rank.

In the words of Shah Ni'matullah:

Mohasebeh, in the beginning, is a balancing of accounts between negative and positive acts. At the end, it is the actualization of pure Unity—in both the station of Unity in multiplicity (being inwardly absorbed in God, while outwardly existing in the world) and Unity in Unity (being outwardly and inwardly absorbed in God).

ورد

VERD

The Sufi Way
of Invocation

NOTE ON TRANSLITERATION

The invocations in this pamphlet are all in the Arabic language. To facilitate recitation the words have been transliterated according to the pronunciation of Persian Moslems. The Latin letters used have their standard pronunciations except for the following:

a   short a as in 'cat'

ā   long a as in 'father'

e   short e as in 'net'

i   long ee as in 'need'

o   long o as in 'row'

u   long oo as in 'food'

ī   long i as in 'idea'

kh   gutteral ch as in Scottish 'loch' or German 'Bach'

q and gh a stopped guttural as if g in 'glove' was pronounced further down in the throat

The symbol ' indicates a glottal stop as in the expelling of breath in the pronunciation of the word 'it'.

O THE ONE WHOSE NAME IS REMEDY

This morning date-wine and sweet sleep at sunrise,
how long will they go on?
Try calling upon God in the dark of night,
and begging his forgiveness at dawn.

Hafez

THE DEFINITION OF VERD

Verd, as defined in the dictionary, means daily work or one's permanent job and duties. It can also signify the prayers that a worshipper repeats every day.

In sufi terminology, verd is the repetition at specified times, with inward purity and the master's permission, of *Qur'anic* verses, Traditions of the Prophet, and particular words or phrases. It involves not only calling upon God, but appealing for forgiveness at his Throne.

103

Although limited in number, some of the verses that occur in the *Qur'an* about verd are as follows:

And so praise God during the night and day that you may find peace. (20:130)

And remember Your Lord's Name in the morning and in the evening. (76:25)

And in the dark of the night prostrate yourself in submission to Him, and praise Him throughout the long night. (76:26)

There were those who slept but little at night.[1] (51:17)

THE SIGNIFICANCE OF VERD

The practice of verd was so significant for some sufi shaikhs that it has been said, "Whoever neglects the practice of verd can have no *vared.*" *Vared* is whatever descends into the sufi's heart without his having to seek or strive for it. It is among the Divine thoughts, there being three kinds of thought: Divine, demonic, and those of the self. Sa'di has said:

In the quiet of night, nothing comes to my heart
more spiritual than Your Vared.

Since in the beginning all sufis find it difficult to be constantly occupied with the remembrance of the heart (*zekr-e qalbi*), and since most sufis feel uncomfortable or become disturbed from this state

---

1. This verse refers to the *mohsenin*—people who were particularly devoted in their spiritual practice, and who spent their nights in the performance of verd and remembrance of the Divine (ed.).

(particularly beginners who lack the capacity for such remembrance), various kinds of verd have been prescribed. Some are bodily like *namaz* (daily prayer), while others are vocal such as *qera'at-e Qur'an* (reading the *Qur'an* aloud) and *tasbih* (invoking the Divine by uttering various words and phrases). Still others are by means of the heart such as *fekr* or *tafakkor* (contemplation). In this way, the sufi's thought remains undisturbed, at each moment having a special occupation. Moreover, it is this variety of moving from one state to another that brings to him stillness and serenity.

At certain points, beginners on the Path may experience a state in which they find it impossible to concentrate upon the remembrance of the heart. While trying to pay attention to their remembrance, they may even observe that their state evolves in such a way as to turn them away from zekr. Thus, at such moments, it is better to concentrate upon the practice of verd until this state passes and the heart again becomes ready to accept zekr.

It is true that shaikhs and perfected ones, from being overwhelmed by the state of Unity, have sometimes preferred silence to verd. However, since no state (*hal*) is stable, they too have returned to the performance of verd after the passing of that state. Other shaikhs, even in the state of Unity, have attempted to maintain the performance of verd. Among these was Jonaid, about whom the following story has been told:

> When Jonaid became old, he still maintained all of the invocations that he had performed in his youth. His disciples finally said to him, "O Shaikh, you have become old, relinquish some of this practice of verd." Jonaid replied, "Whatever I found in the beginning was found through the practice of verd. Thus, it is impossible to abandon such practices at the end.
>
> (Hojwiri, *Kashfo'l-mahjub*)

The principle behind the continuous performance of verd is for the total awareness of the sufi to become centered upon God. As this occurs, his outer and inner being gradually become unified, such that in solitude or among people he is attentive only to Unity. Here, he has become totally absorbed in God, and both his state (*hal*) and his discourse (*qal*) are solely for God and in the service of God.

Reference is made to this process in the prayer of Komail, given to him by his master 'Ali:

> O Lord! I beseech Thee, by Thy pure Essence and Thy greatest Attributes and Names, to keep me in Thy remembrance and service all my days and nights; and to make my actions worthy in Thy sight so that my actions will be in harmony with my words and my state always in Thy service.

THE KINDS OF VERD

1. Namaz (daily prayer)

Sufi shaikhs have traditionally maintained that namaz is the most virtuous kind of verd and the most perfect action that one can perform. Namaz can be divided into two categories:

a. the five required daily prayers of Islam—which should be performed regularly without excuse in accordance with the *shari'at* of Islam.

b. the recommended prayers—which are performed in different states by permission of the master and according to the orders of the *shari'at*.

Some of these recommended prayers are known as *nafeleh* prayers. Each of the five required prayers of Islam has a specific nafeleh prayer associated with it which the master may direct a disciple to recite. 'Shaikhs of the Path' have often stressed the nafeleh prayers associated with the morning and evening namaz. Many of the great shaikhs, however, have considered the nafeleh prayers so important that they have tried not to omit any of them. According to a Sacred Tradition:

> My slave draws ever closer to Me by means of nafeleh prayers until I love him; and when I love him, he comes to

see with My eyes and hear with My ears and speak with My tongue
and grasp with My hand and venture forth with My feet.

2. Verd of the Tariqat

This kind of verd can also be divided into two categories: verds recited after the required prayers and special verds prescribed by the master.

a. Verds Recited after the Required Prayers.

1. After each of the five required prayers, the sufi should recite *Allāho Akbar* 34 times (signifying that nothing can be compared or contrasted to the greatness of God and that God is greater than whatever conception we have of Him), *Alhamdo-lellāh* 33 times (signifying that all praise is God's alone for having brought us into existence from non-existence), and *Sobhānallāh* 33 times (signifying that God is pure from whatever we ascribe to Him).

2. After each of the five required prayers, the sufi should recite 3 or 100 times *Lā elāha ellallāh* ("There is no god but God" . . . who is One, the only One).

3. After each of the five required prayers, the sufi should recite the *Ayato'l-Korsi (Qur'an, 2:255-7)*:

Allāho lā elāha ellā hoval-hayyol-qayyum, lā ta'khozohu senaton va lā nawm. Lahu mā fes-samāvāte va mā fel-arz. Man zallazi yashfa'o 'endahu ella be ezneh. Ya'lamo mā bayna aydihem va mā khalfahom, va lā yohituna be shay'en men 'elmehi ellā be māshā' vase'a korsiyyohus-samāvāte val-arz, va lā ya'odohu hefzahomā, va hoval-'aliyyol-'azim. (255)

Lā ekrāha fed-din, qad tabayyanar-roshdo men al-ghayy, faman yakfor bet-tāghut va yo'men bellāh faqades tamsaka bel-'orvatel-vosqā lanfesāma lahā vallāho sami'un 'alim. (256)

Allāho valiyyollazina āmanu yokhrejohom-men az-zolamāte elan-nur, vallazina kafaru owliya 'ohomot-tāghut, yokhrejunahom men an-nure elaz-zolemāt. Ulā'eka asnābon-nār, hom fihā khāledun. (257)

TRANSLATION

God! There is no god but He, the Living, the Self-Subsistent. Slumber seizes Him not, nor sleep; His are the heavens and the earth. Who is he who may intercede with Him without His permission? He knows what is to come and what has gone before, while they comprehend nothing of His Knowledge but what He wills; His Throne[2] extends over the heavens and the earth, and the preservation of these is no burden for Him; He is the Most Exalted and Great. (255)

There is no compulsion in religion; indeed, the way of Truth is clearly distinguished from the way of error. Hence, he who disbelieves in false deities and believes in God has indeed grasped a strong rope which does not break; verily, God is All-Hearing and All-Knowing. (256)

God is the guide of those who believe; He takes them out of darkness and brings them into the light; but for those who disbelieve, their friends are the rebels (against God) who guide them out of the light and into darkness. They are the companions of the fire wherein they shall abide forever. (257)

4. From being constantly occupied with the practice of verd and various devotional acts, one may gain a sense of pride in one's worship. At such times, the heart becomes overlayed with dust and a very thin veil covers the face of one's thoughts, separating one from God. Thus, after each of the required prayers, the sufi should prostrate himself (in the namaz position of *sajdeh*) and recite the following verd 3, 5, or 7 times—with full concentration, meditation (*moraqebeh*) of the heart, and attention to God:

2. *Korsi:* literally "chair" or "throne," but signifying "authority," "power," "knowledge" (ed.).

Yā mofatteha'l-abvāob, yā mosabbeba'l-asbāb, yā moqallebal-
qolubeval-absār, yā modabberal-laye van-nahār, yā mohav-
velal-hāle val-'ahvāl, havvel hāli elā ahsanel-hāl.

TRANSLATION

O Opener of the doors of grace, O Source of all desires, O
Transformer of hearts and eyes, O Maintainer of night and day,
O Changer of forces and states, change my state to the best of
all states.[3]

5. It is better that the sufi recite the following *qonut* prayer (i.e.
the prayer said during the second rak'at of namaz with the
hands in front of the face):

Allāhomma navver zāheri be tā'ateka, va bāteni be
mahab-bateka va qalbi be ma'refateka va ruhi be
moshāhadateka va serri be'esteqlāle ettesāle hazrateka,
yā zol-jalāle val-ekrām.

Allāhomm-aj'al qalbi nuran va sam'i nuran va basari
nuran va lesāni nuran va yadayya nuran va rejlayya
nuran va jami'a javārehi nuran, yā nural-anvār.

Allāhomma aranal-ashyā'a kamāhi.

Allāhomma kon vajhati fi kolle vajhen, va maqsadi fi
kolle qasden, va ghāyati fi kolle sa'ien, va malje'i va
malāzi fi kolle sheddaten va hammen va vakili fi kolle
amren va tavallani tavallia'enāyaten va mahabbaten fi
kolle hālen. Va sallallāh 'alā mohammaden va ālehi
khayre ālen.

TRANSLATION

O God, illuminate my outer being with obedience to
You, and my inner being with loving-kindness for You,
and my heart with direct knowledge of You, and my
spirit with intimate vision of You, and my essence with

---

3. This section (#4) has been adapted from the *Kebrit-e Ahmar* of
Mozaffar Ali-Shah Kermani, one of the past masters of the Nimatullahi Order.

the ability to reach Thy Throne. O Glorious and Exalted One!

O God, illuminate my heart and my ears and my eyes and my tongue and my hands and my feet and my entire body. O Light of all Lights!

O God, show me things as they truly are.

O God, wherever I turn, be before me; in whatever direction I go, be my destination; in every endeavor of mine, be my aim; in times of difficulty and sorrow, be my refuge and support; in every undertaking, be my advocate; and through Thy Grace and Loving-kindness, take up my actions in Thy Strength.

God's greetings be upon Mohammad and his family, the noblest of all families.

Bayazid had an especially pure and beautiful *qonut:* Elāhi antā ta'lamo mā norid. ("O My Lord, Thou knowest what I want!")

b. Verds Prescribed by the Master at Certain Times and in Specific Repetitions

1. Lā elāha ellā antā, sobhānaka enni konto men az-zālemin. ("There is no god but Thou. Glory be unto Thee; verily I was among the unjust." *Qur'an,* 21:88) Recited 110 times.

This verd is known as *Yunossiyeh* (pertaining to Jonah), for it is said that the Prophet Jonah, by reciting this verd, was released from the belly of the fish of the body in the dark ocean of nature, and admitted to the spiritual realm.

The sufi's view here is that the rational self, like Jonah, is entangled in the darkness of nature, the material world, and the dark desert of the body. Through the assistance of this verd, one becomes attentive to the Unity of God and His Absolute Uniqueness, realizing one's total helplessness and inability. In this way, God comes to set one free from the traps of the material world and sheds upon one the lights of the *shari'at, tariqat,* and *haqiqat.*

2. Yā hayyo yā qayyum, yā man lā elāha ellā antā,
berahmatekā estaghis. (O Thou, Alive and Ever-Lasting; O
Thou, there is no god but Thou; I take refuge in Thy Grace.)
Recited 41 times.

3. Sobhānallāhe va behamdehi, sobhānallāhe l-'azime va
behamdehi, astaghforollāh. (God is pure and all praise is God's!
Pure is the Great God, and all praise is God's alone. I seek
forgiveness from Him.) Recited 100 times.

4. Qol allāhomma mālekal-molk, to'teyal-molka man tashā, va
tanze'ol-molka memman tashā, va to'ezzo man tashā, va tozello
man tashā. Beyadakal-khar. Ennaka 'alā kolle shay'en qadir.
Tulejol-layle fin-nahār, va tulejon-nahāra fil-layl, va tokhrejol-
hayya men al-mayyet, va tokhrejol-mayyeta men al-hayy, va
tarzoqo man tashā'o beghayre hesāb. ("Say, 'O God, Possessor
of the kingdom, Thou bestowest the kingdom upon whomever
Thou willest, and Thou removest the Kingdom from whomever
Thou willest; Thou endearest whomever Thou willest, and Thou
disgracest whomever Thou willest; the good is in Thy Hand and
verily Thou art mighty over all things; Thou turnest night into
day, and day into night; Thou bringest forth the living out of
the dead, and the dead out of the living; and Thou givest
sustenance to whomever Thou willest without measure.' "
Qur'an, 3:25-6) Recited 22 times.

5. Besmellāher-rahmāner-rahim, lā hawla va lā qovvata ellā
be'llāhel-aliyel-azim. (In the Name of God, the Merciful and
Compassionate, there is no force and power but in God, the
Most Exalted and Great.) Recited 7 times.

6. Hovallāholazi lā elāha ellā hu, 'ālemol-ghaibe vash-shahā-
date, hovar-rahmānor-rahim. (He is God, there is no god but
He—the Knower of the unseen and seen; He is the Merciful and
the Compassionate.) Recited 7 times.

7. Hovallāholazi lā elāha ellā hoval-malekol-qoddusos-sal-
āmol-mo'menol-mohaymenol-'azizo'l-jabbāro'l-motakabber.
Sobhānallāhe 'ammā yoshre-kun. ("He is God, there is no god
but He; He is the Pure King, free from defect, the Provider of

112   refuge, the Dear Guardian, the Omnipotent, the Supreme!
Hallowed is God from whatever they associate (with Him)."
Qur'an, 59:23)

8.   Hovallāhol-khāleqol-bāri'ol-mosavver,   lahol-asmā'   ol-
hosnā.   Yosabbeho lahu mā fes-samāvāte val-arz.   Va hoval-
'azizol-hakim. ("He is God, the Conceiver, the Creator, the
Maker, the Fashioner; His are all the Virtuous Names; everything in the heavens and the earth calleth upon Him; He is the
Cherished, the All-Wise." *Qur'an*, 59:24)

THE RECITATION OF QUR'ANIC VERSES

Whenever the opportunity or inclination arises, the sufi may
repeat any of the following *Qur'anic* verses:

1.   Va'elāhokom elāhon vāhedon, lā elāha ellā hovar-rahmānor-rahim.

"And your God is one God! There is no god but He; He is
the Merciful, the Compassionate." (*Qur'an*, 2:163)

2.   Shahedallāh annahu lā elāha ellā hu, val-malā'ekato va
ulul-'elme qa'eman bel-qest, lā elāha ellā hoval-'azizol-hakim.

"God (Himself) witnesseth that there is no god but He, and
so do the angels and those possessed of knowledge, who stand
firm for Divine Justice and Oneness; there is no god but He, the
Cherished and All-Wise." (3:17)

3.   Zālekomollāho rabbokom, lā elāha ellā hu, khāleqo kolle
shay'an fa'boduhu va hova 'alā kolle shay'an vakil.

"There is your God, your Lord; there is no god but He, the
Creator of all things; therefore worship Him; He is the guardian
over all things." (6:103)

4.   Fa'en tavvalāw faqol hasbiyallāh-ho, lā elāha ellā hova
alayhe tavakalto va hova rabbol-'arshel-'azim.

"If they (the enemies) turn away, say thou: 'God is sufficient unto me; there is no god but He; on Him do I rely, and He is the Lord of the Glorious Throne.' " (9:129)

5. Va'en tajhar bel-qawle fa'ennahu ya'lamos-serra va akhfā. Allāho lā elāha ellā hu, lahol-asmā'ol-hosnā.

"And whether thou revealest it by speaking or not, He knowest the secret and the hidden; God, there is no god but He; His are the Virtuous Names." (20:7-8)

6. Ennamā elāh-hokomollāh allazi, lā elāha ellā hu, vase'a kolle shay'an 'elmā.

"Verily, your God is the only God; there is no god but He; He comprehendeth all things by His Knowledge." (20:98)

7. Fata'ālallāhol-malekol-haqq, lā elāha ellā hu, rabbol-'arshel karim.

"Then the most Exalted is God, the True King; there is no god but He, the Lord of the Throne of Generosity. (23:116)

8. Allāho lā elāha ellā hova rabbol-'arshel-'azim.

"God, there is no god but He! He is the Lord of the Glorious Throne." (27:26)

9. Va hovallāho lā elāha ellā hu, lahol-hamdo fel-ulā val-ākherat va lahul-hokm va elayhe torja'un.

"And He is God; there is no god but He! All praise is His, in this world and the world hereafter; His is the Authority, and unto Him shall ye be returned." (28:70)

10. Va lā tad'o ma'allāhe elāhan ākhara, lā elāha ellā hu, kollo shay'en hālekun ellā vajhah lahul-hokm va elayhe torja'un.

"And invoke not with God any other god; there is no god but He; all things are perishable but His Face; His is the Authority and unto Him shall ye be returned." (28:88)

114   11. Hoval-hayy lā elāha ellā hu, fad'uhu mokhlesina lahod-din, al-hamdo lillāhe rabbel-'ālemin.

"He is the Living; there is no god but He; so call unto Him, devoting unto Him the religion; all praise is God's, the Lord of both worlds." (40:65)

12. Allāho lā elāha ellā hu, va'alallāhe falyatavakkalel-mo'menun.

"God, there is no god but He; and upon God the faithful trust." (64:13)

13. Rabbol-mashreqe val-maghreb, lā elāha ellā hu, fa'takhez-ho vakilā.

"The Lord of east and west, there is no god but He; therefore take Him as your Advocate." (73:9)

NOTE: Conditions permitting, disciples are given permission to study the *Qur'an*, particularly Suras 56 (*Al-Waqi'ah*) and 67 (Al-Mulk).

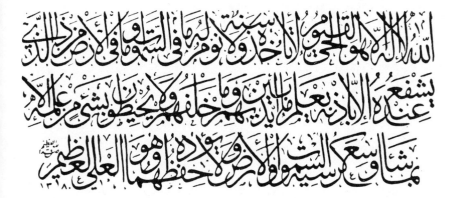

Ayato'l-Korsi (Qur'an, 2:255)

آداب ورود در سلك صوفیان

THE RULES
AND
MANNERS
OF INITIATION
INTO
THE SUFI PATH

LOVE'S SECRETS

The time of separation and sadness, pain and burning
*   has passed.*
The illumined moon and firmament have become as desired.

Now, in the True Friend's district, we're drunk and ruined.
We endure the dregs of pain at night and by daylight drink wine.

I tell Him, if You are still going to torment me, speak up.
He says, there's still more blame and difficulty to come.

Flowing tears and the heart's breast-burning sigh
*   did no good.*
Nothing worked but the kindness of the Beloved.

Spiritual state and ecstasy gave us not a moment's peace—
As if autumn and summer were also spring.

I'm praising the honor of the tavern of ruin, since
*   out of respect*
Both king and rag-mender kiss its threshold.

Nurbakhsh, why are you telling Love's secrets so openly?
Where Love is, there are no secrets.

هو

Enter not into the 'Tavern of Ruin'
without observing its manners,
For the dwellers at its door
are the confidants of the King.

Hafez

Entering the path of the people of the heart involves observing certain 'rules and manners' (*adab*) and ceremonies which for centuries have been respected and adhered to by sufis. These 'rules and manners' and ceremonies have been handed down and followed by the 'shaikhs of the Path' up to the present time.

In view of the command, ''Travel the Path in the way that others have traveled the Path before,'' these 'rules and manners' have been enumerated herein and their secrets and meanings explained so that this work may be a guide for seekers.

THE FIVE GHOSLES [1]

Before being initiated into the world of Spiritual Poverty (*faqr*), those who seek to travel towards God must first perform *niyat* [2] and then five *ghosles* in the manner described below:

1. *ghosle:* the act of ablution—washing of the whole body in a prescribed manner for the purpose of purification (ed).

2. *niyat:* a vow or declaration of one's intention to perform a particular devotional act (most commonly, namaz or daily prayer) (ed).

119

1. Ghosle of Repentance (tobeh)

With this ghosle, the seeker repents from his or her former misdoings and strayings. He or she also apologizes, when becoming joined to the worship of God, for the previous sin of self-worship.

2. Ghosle of Submission (Islam)

In the ghosle of submission, the seeker who is not already a Moslem makes a vow (*niyat*) to accept Islam and become a Moslem. If one is already a Moslem by tongue or tradition, one vows to become commited with heart and spirit (*ruh*) to the holy *shari'at* of Islam and to behave in agreement with its orders.

In accordance with the saying of 'Ali, "Islam is surrendering," the seeker should surrender himself fully to God's Will, both outwardly and inwardly, and be content with whatever God desires.

3. Ghosle of Initiation into Spiritual Poverty (faqr)

To enter into the world of Spiritual Poverty, one must be pure both outwardly and inwardly. Thus, one performs ghosle outwardly and cleanses the outer being so that the inner being will also incline towards purity.

> *Purify thyself, then proceed to the 'Tavern of Ruin'*
> *that it not be polluted by you.*
>
> *Hafez*

4. Ghosle of Pilgrimage (ziyarat)

It is a tradition when visiting people of respect in the world to cleanse one's body and put on clean clothes. Similarly, when making a pilgrimage to the Perfected One, or 'Master of the Path' (*pir-e tariqat*), one should be cleansed and purified in the same way.

Hafez

For this reason, the seeker performs ghosle, cleansing the outer being, before approaching the master to acquire the orders of the Path.

5. Ghosle of Fulfillment (qaza-ye hajat)

Since the 'supplication' (*niyaz*) of the seeker in traveling along the Path is to reach the rank of the Perfected One, a ghosle for the fulfillment of this aim is performed before coming into the master's presence.

THE FIVE SYMBOLS OF SPIRITUAL POVERTY

After the seeker has performed the five ghosles, he or she prepares five objects which are taken together into the master's presence and given to him so that the master may accept and guide the seeker on the path of the travelers of Unity. These five objects are: a few yards of white cloth, a whole nutmeg, a ring, a coin, and some rock candy. Each of these objects is symbolic of a certain commitment made by the one who seeks to travel towards God. These commitments are represented by objects so that they will remain fixed in the traveler's mind and never be forgotten.

1. White Cloth (chelvar)

The white cloth taken into the master's presence represents the traveler's shroud and indicates that the traveler, like a dead body in the hands of a *ghasal* (one who washes the dead), surrenders himself fully to God. In doing so, he (or she) considers the master's orders as God's orders and obeys them without questioning "how" or "why".

2. Whole Nutmeg (joz)

Joz represents the head of the traveler. In presenting *joz* to the master, the traveler consents to never reveal the Divine secrets that are confided in him or her. Even if threatened with decapitation, one should not reveal such secrets. In other words, the traveler's head is symbolically presented to the master here as a hostage for God's secrets.

3. Ring (angoshtar)

The ring given to the master upon entering the world of Spiritual Poverty represents the band worn by slaves in olden times and signifies the traveler's devotion to God. In presenting this ring to the master, the traveler vows to become devoted solely to God and to give up the desire for anything else.

4. Coin (sekkeh)

The coin symbolizes the wealth and riches of the world. The traveler, in presenting this coin to the master or shaikh, promises to empty the heart of any desire for the wealth of the world. Here, it should be noted, the object is to have no *attachment* to wealth. If the sufi is rich one day, then poor the next, he remains unaffected by either condition. In the state of richness, the sufi should be generous; in the state of poverty, joyful and patient.

5. Rock Candy (nabat)

Nabat represents the candy given as an offering at the second birth of the seeker. Whereas the seeker's first birth is from his or her mother, the second birth comes upon entering the domain of Spiritual Poverty. With this re-birth, the seeker steps into the realm of Spirituality, Truth, and Unification, being born from the mother of nature and multiplicity into the world of Love (*eshq*), Loving-kindness (*mohabbat*), and Unity (*tawhid*).

In presenting this rock candy, the traveler also comes to realize that the Path should be traversed with peace of mind and gladness, not with depression and displeasure.

THE FIVE COMMITMENTS

Before entering into the circle of Spiritual Poverty, the seeker makes five commitments to the master. It is only when the seeker accepts and understands the significance of these commitments that the master comes to guide him or her along the straight path of Unity of the Nimatullahi Order.

1. Obedience to the Holy Shari'at of Mohammad, the Seal of the Prophets

The seeker, upon entering the world of the sufis, makes a commitment to obey the 'rules and manners' (*adab*) of the *shari'at* of Islam. If he or she has not already been a Moslem, the two testimonies of Islam (*shahadatain*) should be uttered here. These are: "I testify that there is no god but God" (*Ashhado an la elaha ella'llah*) and "I testify that Mohammad is His Prophet" (*Ashhado anna Mohammadan rasulo'llah*). The seeker then adds, "I testify that 'Ali is the Saint of God" (*Ashhado anna 'Aliyan valiyo'llah*). In so declaring, the seeker accepts with heart and spirit (*ruh*) the truth and spirituality of Islam which is the acceptance of the Absolute Sainthood of 'Ali—the King of all Saints. At this point, the seeker makes the commitment not to neglect the orders of the *shari'at* of Islam.

2. Kindness towards God's Creatures

With this commitment, the sufi vows never to bother and to be kind and friendly towards all of God's creatures while traveling on the Path. Here, the sufi should constantly put into practice the words of Sa'di's poem which states:

I am joyful and content in the world,
for the world is joyful and content from Him.
I am in love with all of the universe,
for all of the universe belongs to Him.

3. Preservation of the Secrets of the Path

At the beginning of traveling on the Path (*soluk*), the sufi makes a commitment not to reveal to anyone the secrets he or she is told—regardless of whether the person is a stranger, friend, or fellow darvish. These secrets consist of the remembrance and contemplation he or she is given, as well as all discoveries and revelations witnessed in the world of Unity. Such secrets should be spoken of to no one but the master. In this way, the secret will not fall into the hands of one unable to keep it.

That friend from whom the top of the gallows
became honored
Was the one accused of revealing the secrets.

Hafez

4. Service on the Path

From the beginning to the end of traveling on the Path, the sufi must undertake to accept and obey with heart and spirit, and without questioning "how" and "why", every order and service that is given by the master. The sufi should know that acting carelessly in such service will only cause one to stray from the path of devotion and the straight path. So effective is such service that it can be said, "Whatever the sufi finds, he has found from service."

Sa'di presents a beautiful illustration of service in his poem from the *Bustan* about Sultan Mahmud and Ayaz, the Sultan's servant. The poem begins with someone criticising Mahmud by saying, "What

wonder this is! Ayaz, his favorite, has no beauty. A flower without
color, without any smell, how strange is the nightingale's attraction!"
When told of these words, Mahmud replies, "Truly my love is upon
his virtue, and not on his form or his face."

Sa'di then proceeds to recount the story of how in a royal
procession a camel laden with jewels and pearls once stumbled and
fell, spilling its precious stones. Sultan Mahmud, being generous, gave
permission for his followers to plunder the jewels and hastily rode
away. All of the followers broke rank and rushed to gather the jewels,
neglecting the King for this wealth. Only Ayaz ignored the jewels and
followed after the King. When Mahmud saw him following, he called
out, "O Ayaz, what has thou gained of the plunder?" In reply, Ayaz
declared, "I sought no jewels, but followed my King; for how can I
occupy myself with your gifts when all I seek is to serve?"

Sa'di then concludes:

> O friend, if you become near to the Throne,
>> neglect not the King for His jewels;
> For on this path, the saint never asks
>> anything of God but Him.
> So know if you seek but the grace of the Friend,
>> you're entangled in your prison, not His.

5. Deeg-jush

Upon entering the world of Spiritual Poverty, the sufi declares
inwardly, "I have come in order to sacrifice myself for the Friend."

To demonstrate this, just as Abraham by God's command
sacrificed a sheep instead of Ishmael, the sufi should prepare a special
meal made from a sheep in accordance with the *adab* and traditions of
Spiritual Poverty and distribute it among the darvishes. The food so
prepared is called *deeg-jush*.

أعداء فألّف بين قلوبكم فأصبحتم بنعمته إخوانًا

قال الله تعالى واذكروا نعمة الله عليكم كنتم

Allah, the Supreme, says . . . remember the grace
and blessings of Allah (*ni'matullah*) upon you:
you were stubborn enemies and He joined your hearts
in love, so that by His grace and blessings
you have become brothers and sisters.